(Re)MAKING LOVE:
a sex after sixty story

By Mary L. Tabor

Outer Banks Publishing Group
Outer Banks • Raleigh

Second Edition
eISBN-13 978-1-4524-9694-8
ISBN-10 098299317X
ISBN-13 978-0-9829931-7-0

July 2011

Praise for (Re)MAKING LOVE

(Re)Making Love - A love story for any age, August 15, 2010

By K. Mayfield (London, England) ○○○○○

Mary Tabor's (Re)Making Love is one of the best memoirs I've read in quite a long while - and I've read more than a few. I found myself fiercely cheerleading her on as she fought her way through an unwanted separation from her husband of 21 years. Her writing is smart, funny, lyrical and at times, heartbreaking.

How many times have you read a blurb that used the words "unflinchingly honest" when describing a memoir? I always say to myself, well of course, shouldn't it be? But often they are not. (Re)Making Love is that - and more. Mary puts beauty into ugly honesty, laughter into sad honesty and hope into painful honesty.

There is even a surprise ending!

I highly recommend this book.

Another Beautiful Book from Mary Tabor, August 10, 2010

By Kyle Minor "reader" (Columbus, Ohio) ○○○○○

Here is a book that stretches the promise of the lyric essay to book length, and the result, for the reader, is at least sixty-seven varieties of pleasure. (Re)Making Love is intelligent, occasionally heartbreaking, and ultimately inspiring. And, I almost forgot: Sexy. I want to be like Mary Tabor when I grow up.

Wonderful Story, August 10, 2010

By mdalton322 ○○○○○

Mary Tabor, starts her excellent book with a reference to the movie Charade, and ends with an equally effective metaphor from the same movie. There is nothing about Mary's insightful memoir that is a charade, of course, and that is just part of what makes (Re)Making Love a book that is deserving of the reader's attention. Mary Tabor has written a memoir that removes the veil from who we are as people, and who we are as people in relationships. There is no charade in the search for who one truly is, the writer knows this; a remarkable achievement in an age when the existential search for the soul has been mitigated to cliché adventures in a dark and stormy night. There is nothing cliché about what Mary Tabor has written and there is nothing cliché about the desire to understand the connection, the longing of romance and desire, that one person has with another person. Her story is wholly unique beautiful and imaginative. Not only has Mary remade love in her novel, she has remade the medium in which an author can communicate with her audience. (Re)Making Love: started as a blog and has been made, or remade, into a wonderful book that all should read. The work itself is a remaking of how we conceive of the memoir and how we remove the charade from our self.

A Story of True Love, January 16, 2011
By Wart ♢♢♢♢♢
Mary has shared with us in her book, "(Re)Making Love: A Sex After Sixty Story" that with hope love and forgiveness that everything is possible. I found her story uplifting as I go through my personal journey in life. It made me realize that those people who truly love you will forgive you, stand by you and support you always. Most of all there is always hope. Mary shows us that by living life and facing its challenges we grow and become better even from our personal failures. A true love story you must read with a real life happy ever after ending.

The Best Is Yet to Come, August 27,2010
By D. A. Hickman (Indianapolis) ♢♢♢♢♢
Mary L. Tabor is charting new territory with her lovely memoir RL:SASS. Her story proves that beginnings occur in our lives at any age, that change comes when least expected and somehow we must endure and thrive. Her story is our story: indeed, a universal story of transition, finding peace, and discovering life anew. This is a book to read slowly, appreciating the subtle and the not-so-subtle. If you are looking for a kindred spirit, look no further. Women the world

over will enjoy this book, regardless of age, location, personal circumstances. I'm hoping to watch her guest appearance on Oprah. Are you listening, Oprah?

From T.S. Eliot to The Wizard of Oz, Mary Tabor's Great Read, October 24, 2010 ♧♧♧♧♧
By Seymour M. Nemirow
Nietzsche and T.S. Eliot created hope and beauty in the face of modern despair. Mary Tabor has woven their prose and poetry into her own finely textured reflections on the near despair of lost loved ones--one dearly loved human being after another, early in life. Not enough: The fates lash one more stone around her neck; the love of her life loves her but insists they live apart, which they do.
How can the reader, not to mention the author, go on with her life or this book? I put the book down. Can I handle such tragedy, sadness? Yet there was something quite engaging between the lines, pulling me in. As the days and weeks passed, I found her story increasingly engaging, eloquent, witty. Written with high intellect. And using, film buff that she is, a kind of indirect lighting illuminating her life--romcom films, fairly tales, dreams, N.Y. Times headlines.
Tabor began a blog interacting with readers a few years ago. She highly respects her readers. It showed in her blog and now in the book, enhanced by lovely graphics, photos, tighter continuity and clearer context. Her emotional journey made me root for her one day, mock her the next, finally suspend judgment as she wove a tale postmodern yet romantic, Four Quartets and Hollywood, existential angst and quantum mechanics, why lovers cheat and why Christmas in Paris is a magic show. Above all we are detectives, partners with this Sam Spade (I'm showing my age) investigating who if anyone is guilty, and will be the next sentence, so to speak. The passion for her and us is in the search. Read it.
Martin Nemirow
Former book reviewer, Hartford Courant, Los Angeles Times

Memoir as poetry, January 18, 2011
By DCer (Washington, DC USA) ♧♧♧♧♧
When I bought Mary Tabor's, (Re)Making Love: A Sex After Sixty Story, I had certain expectations about the book, and I was not disappointed. But I got more -- much more -- than I expected. I discovered that this memoir had a punch to it and transcended its own subject. It has subtle levels of complexity that I'm still discovering as I reread it.
There's no doubt that this is indeed the story of a woman in her sixties

suddenly cut loose from her moorings, and her sometimes tragic, sometimes funny, road to finding love and herself again. The book is interspersed with literary references and some unlikely things (hint: has to do with cooking). It's also richly entertaining. Mary tells her story courageously and with breathtaking candor, and a surface reading of the book will be very enjoyable and rewarding.

But a deeper reading of the book -- beyond the plot -- will yield more, where you will discover themes and insights that Mary did not always consciously intend to reveal. This, though, is the stuff of great literature and writing, where the greatest insights are often gleaned and discerned by the reader who dares to plumb the psyche of the writer. It is through this that we internalize her experiences, recognizing and discovering ourselves, not just for how we have responded to life's crises, but how we might. There are cautionary tales here (e.g., Internet dating) that may just influence some readers on how not to react in a crisis.

Daisy Hickman, of the SunnyRoomStudio blog, interviewed Mary last October and characterized (Re)Making Love as a "living memoir." This is not as obvious as it seems. Mary began her book as a blog, writing about events as they unfurled and whirled. In the epilogue in her book, she writes that her daughter and son-in-law suggested that ". . . I write about my journey while I lived it. They said 'Blog,' while I wept, and I did." Thus, it is indeed a living memoir, full of uncensored, raw emotions and the stumbles and falls during her journey.

Yet, it's still more than that. Mary's exquisite writing skill infuses her memoir with poetic qualities. If you approach it this way, it will enhance your reading experience.

The book begins at the end-- the end of her marriage. In Chapter One, "I Need to Live Alone," -- the roundelay of her memoir -- Mary lays it out in stark simplicity: "I had been married twenty-one years when D. [her husband] announced, 'I need to live alone.' Oh so Greta Garbo. There was absolutely no noise." Announced; just like that.

From there Mary takes us on her journey, reaching back to her childhood, her losses of family, her gaining of family, her courtship with D. and the aftermath of the Announcement.

Thus, this is a book that I took in portions so that I could absorb more. In one particularly intimate and poignant chapter, "Deceptive Cadence," Mary skillfully weaves in Shubert's Opus 90, No. 3, in G Flat, which has much to do with "D." The three short pages of the chapter stopped me flat in my tracks. I had to read it again, but first downloaded the piece, and then played it while I read it. I was deeply moved-- more than I expected. I suggest the same for other readers; the results are palpable. I learned later that Mary wrote the chapter in cadence to the piece.

While Mary became unmoored, she did not become unhinged. She made mistakes and sometimes reckless decisions with the best of intentions: (Re)making love and getting off that awful island of Lost. She attributes her not completely losing it not to herself, but to her metaphoric passport. In the chapter, "The Last Place You Look," she writes:

"Here's how I think of my passport: On the front is a picture of my father. My picture lies under his and under my mother's. Remembering from where I've come has helped. My father's love, my childhood with them lay inside that passport to my destination."

And her children and their families helped too by keeping her under close watch, oftentimes helplessly as they learned of some of her missteps (essentially always with men), but their entreaties sometimes fell on deaf ears. Mary channeled the teenager within.

But while Mary is taken advantage of and sometimes mistreated in this book, she's no victim, nor ever invokes that role. She knows what she's doing and the risks she's taking. And she takes action when it's necessary. One particularly delicious instance is when a suitor, m.r.s., a widower "still married" as Mary soon learns, dumps her (in an email, of course) after a briefly promising start. He writes that he feels "badly" about doing this. A badly chosen word, "badly," to use with a professional writer. Her parting shot is searing. No spoilers here. Read it in the chapter, "I'm Cooked."

The book transcends itself because a deep reading of it reveals lessons and insights that affects all of us, regardless of age or gender. I bought copies for my two adult sons, as I wanted them to get their own unique experiences out of it.

As one of Mary's readers wrote of (Re)Making Love, "(Mary's) experiences and the way she brings them to us remind us why we bother to read in the first place . . ." At the end of a video interview posted on her website, Mary says so modestly of (Re)Making Love, "I hope it's worth your time." It is; it is. Her courageous -- and funny, insightful, thought-provoking, shocking and soothing --memoir is so well worth our time.

In closing, it's notable that Mary quotes Nietzsche often, and in Chapter 10, "Bliss," she informs us that Nietzsche uses the term "bliss" 26 times in Thus Spoke Zarathustra. (No, she had not found it then.) Nietzsche also used the term "joy" many times (from the German "lust," not in the common English usage, but rather as an active, participative joy). In Nietzsche's book is the famous poem "Zarathustra's Roundelay," where joy is used very hopefully:

O man, take care!
What does the deep midnight declare?
"I was asleep--
From a deep dream I woke and swear:
The world is deep,
Deeper than day had been aware.
Deep is its woe;
Joy--deeper yet than agony:
Woe implores: Go!
But all joy wants eternity--
Wants deep, wants deep eternity."

This joy Mary does find and continues to experience. You can experience it with her by not just reading, but absorbing this transformational book.

Oh, the paradox . . . January 27, 2011

By R. Pluta 👐👐👐👐👐

Mary's well-written emotional story is a must-read for people who appreciate intelligence and all the good things in life.

The author takes us on a curve-filled tale accompanied with poetry, movies, art, music, food (with recipes), nostalgia and reminiscences both sweet and sour.

As with all masterful compositions, this one holds treasure greater than what the title alone suggests. Some people report reading the book at one sitting. However, this book is meant to be savored over time with the knowledge that all journeys have a beginning and an ending. When it's over, you'll want more.

Refreshingly Romantic, February 1, 2011

By annaliz 👐👐👐👐👐

Heartache and the brothers Grimm, loss and John Donne, the salving grace of the romantic comedy - Mary Tabor intelligently interweaves the fragments of a broken heart in her memoir, "(Re)Making Love." The effect is a distinctly affecting love story, where to read Mary is to wish your best friend had the author's wealth of allusions always at her disposal, or Mary's elegance with a phrase. Although her story of love lost and found has a well-tread tradition behind it, like a good romantic comedy, it's the experience of indulging in "Love" that proves an unparalleled joy for the reader looking to lose her (or him)self in one romantic's unapologetic search for the fulfillment that yes, you'll come to declare, she deserves. References to online dating and modern films may place the tale firmly in the 21st-century, but one of the work's more endearing qualities is its equally firm rejection of 21st-century irony (no Mary, don't ever become more `ironized'). Hipsters may moan over our inability to connect in a world where the threat of a disconnected laptop, BlackBerry or Smartphone spells disaster - Mary, no less "modern," is able to indulge without the whine, touching on clichés without ever becoming one herself. LOVE is one of the most difficult concepts, sentiments, burdens a writer can choose to tackle so directly, and consequently, the most unfailingly popular. Mary, in her fearlessness, has advanced the challenge to expert level - not only does she dare write about LOVE, but does so earnestly. Before or after 60, the earnest reader will respond to this recognition of kind, finding his or her own satisfaction, alongside the author, in "Love." I HIGHLY recommend it!

A Feast of a Book, May 11, 2011

By KatyO "books books books" (Galway, Eire) 🌀🌀🌀🌀🌀

My review does not have the greatest title, but here's what I mean - Mary L. Tabor's '(Re)Making Love: A Sex After Sixty Story' is one of those books that you just have to read twice.

The first to be gobbled in one sitting, quickly, eagerly, willing the outcome to be a good one (and it is).

The second, to take time over, slowly and softly reveling in her marvelous writing. What a writer!

People often say that truth is stranger than fiction, and so it is in the case of this memoir.

The author's self shines through as she tells her tale without the slightest hint of self-pity, admirable indeed under such a set of circumstances.

What's more, she mixes and spices and weaves a story interlaced with fairy tales, movies, recipes and dreams. And the result is a truly inspirational book - moving, intimate, philosophical, elegant and honest.

I really loved reading this, and you will too.

For my mother, my father and my sister, who would have helped if they'd known.

Table of Contents

Prologue

For this second edition that comes now one year after its first publication, I would like to share with you as you embark on the journey of *(Re)Making Love* what I have learned about living within time's limits from writing this book and from living beyond its first publication. Rabbi Hillel, who spoke these words 2,000 years ago, has been widely quoted ever since, perhaps most notably in my lifetime by the ilk of Primo Levi and Robert F. Kennedy.

If I am not for myself, then who will be for me? And if I am only for myself, then what am I? And if not now, when?

Truly *knowing* what these words mean has come from the place of *not knowing*. And by this I mean that I have had to live this journey without the full understanding of their plain spoken sense. I have had to learn the hard way: through the good, the bad and the foolish that this memoir recounts.

Mary

Mary L. Tabor
July 2011

I Need to Live Alone

I love romantic comedies: weep over them, quote their dialogue without attribution in conversation as when I am with a man who says he wants to be friends with me, "You actually believe that men and women can be friends?"

When Harry Met Sally: Harry: "What I'm saying is—and this is not a come-on in any way, shape, or form—is that men and women can't be friends, because the sex part always gets in the way."

I collect music scores of Rom-Coms, buy the DVDs and watch them over and over again. Now sure, the appeal to me and others is this: girl meets boy and LOVE results, inexorable, indomitable, irrefutable, life-changing LOVE.

I was sixty years old when my husband—let's refer to him as D.—dumped me—old story, I know. But wait, as the commercials for fancy French Fry cutters say.

I begin writing about my separation from D. on August 25, my parents' anniversary. They were married fifty-four years. Can you believe it? I am alone and reading *The New York Times* in my condo where I live now. I find this: AP report, dateline: Chamonix, France (Isn't that where Cary meets Audrey in *Charade's* first scene? "Can't he do something constructive like start an avalanche or something?" Reggie, played by Audrey Hepburn asks Silvie after young Jean Louis shoots her in the face with his water gun. Jean Louis shoots

Peter, played by Cary Grant, as well.) The AP reports on an avalanche that "swept down a major summit in the French Alps before dawn on Sunday, leaving eight climbers missing and presumed dead along a trail often used to reach Mont Blanc . . . One survivor, Marco Delfini, an Italian guide, said he saw 'a wall of ice coming towards us, and then we were carried 200 meters.' An injured survivor Nicholas Duquesnes, told Agence France-Presse, 'There was absolutely no noise; it was very disturbing. We only had time to swerve to the right before being mowed down.' "

I had been married twenty-one years when D. announced, "I need to live alone." Oh so Greta Garbo. There was absolutely no noise. I was sixty years old and had been chasing him around the bedroom—to no avail—for ten years. Bill Maher in a comedy routine on HBO not so long after he had been dumped by ABC only to arise again with *Politically Incorrect*, said in a joke about older women, "menopause." Get it? Men A Pause. Yeah, I got it.

The French Fry Cutter salesman raises his voice on the commercial in my head: "But wait, there's more": I decide to date. I want a man who believes that men and women in love *must* be friends. But Harry is right that the sex part matters.

The hell with Bill Maher.

The Princess and Her House

But first, we sell our house—against my wishes—and I buy a condo in the Penn Quarter of DC.

I live a short walk from the White House. It's on my route to my teaching job at George Washington University. As I write this and look back to 2006 when my life fell apart, Michelle and Barack Obama live in the House. Go to *The Daily Green (thedailygreen.com)* to see a picture of the beautiful princess Michelle in her garden on the south lawn of the White House. A princess should live in a white house. She says, "Every single person from Prince Charles on down was excited we are planting a garden."

I live in the condo I bought when D. and I sold the old lady of a house in Adams Morgan. But I was not there for the leaving of the house. I took a cab to the airport and flew to Columbia, Missouri, for a visiting writers job. On the curb stood my daughter Sarah and her husband Ryan and my husband D. In the trunk was the big suitcase with as many clothes and books I could fit. In another truck owned by Town and Country Movers—the moving company that moved us into the house and would move us apart—were all my files, my computer, the chair I sit in now to write at the computer and one stuffed chair from my attic study. I was moving to what I thought was a furnished house.

D. would move the furniture and dishes and paintings and photos we had into our two separate condos two and a half blocks apart. But I would not live in mine for one academic year.

And what an education that year was.

In olden times, when wishing still did some good, there lived a king whose daughters were all beautiful, but the youngest was so beautiful that the sun itself, who, indeed, has seen so much, marveled every time it shone upon her face. In the vicinity of the king's castle there was a large, dark forest, and in this forest, beneath an old linden tree, there was a well. In the heat of the day the princess would go out into the forest and sit on the edge of the cool well.

And so "The Frog-King" begins, and, yes, this is the same story as "The Frog-Prince."

We are in the game of Charades. Two different versions of the same tale: *when wishing still did some good . . .*

In June 2006, two months before I moved to Missouri to teach, two months before the actual physical separation, when our house in Adams Morgan was sold and I moved out of town, I made up a vignette:

Dreamlike.

In this less-than-perfect perfect town where the husbands take their bikes to the train or their wives pick them up in cars, where the storefronts have signs that say things like Simply Good or Hats Galore or Pink and Blue, the dream of adultery understood unfolds: Lily is having an affair with Gordon, her best friend's husband. During a party that this friend, Skilly, is having, Lilly sits on Gordon's lap. The adulterous pair Gordon and Lilly become entwined rapidly whenever they are together. They hide, skulk—a word Lilly heard in a British romantic comedy that describes what they must do to be together. But at the party Skilly can be seen more often than usual with Fergus who is married to Lilly. When Lily leaves the bathroom, she sees Fergus with Skilly, his hand in hers.

Suddenly Lilly knows they are all free.

She tells Gordon, "Skilly and Fergus. Yes, I know you don't believe it, but yes, Skilly and Fergus."

Gordon will ride his bike to the train in the morning but what will he do about Skilly when it is Lilly's vulva that he craves?

Nietzsche says, *But thought is one thing, the deed is another, and the image of the deed still another: the wheel of causality does not roll between them.*

I knew when I made up the vignette that my husband did not want me—or so I thought. I created a fantasy that we would each find other partners and simply exchange.

Do Sa Do. Change partners.

Here is what Dorothy Parker had to say:

General Review of the Sex Situation

> *Woman wants monogamy;*
> *Man delights in novelty.*
> *Love is woman's moon and sun;*
> *Man has other forms of fun.*
> *Woman lives but in her lord;*
> *Count to ten, and man is bored.*
> *With this the gist and sum of it.*
> *What earthly good can come of it?*

I prefer D. H. Lawrence:

> *But firm at the centre*
> *My heart was found;*
> *My own to her perfect*
> *Heartbeat bound,*
> *Like a magnet's keeper*
> *Closing the round.*

Do Sa Do. Change houses.

Here is what I found in August 2006 in Missouri. Consider this a letter I wrote you after I'd arrived:

The furnished house I rented sight unseen turns out to be a pit owned by a tenured English professor and her poet husband—both writers. The first thing I had to do was buy a bed as they were sleeping on a 20-year-old futon and I woke the first night thinking I must be the princess and the pea as a stone is clearly sticking into my hip bone. But it was the futon that has hardened over the years into a substance not unlike cement.

Did you know that when you are desperate and have no car—am getting to that—you can order a bed over the phone? The kitchen did not have a working oven for three weeks: The owners didn't want to fix it—but eventually came around. So as of today I do have an oven, but only three of the four burners on the stove work. The cabinets have virtually no glassware or dishes and every spoon is bent. They didn't even leave me a can opener that works. But they did leave me the trash can in the kitchen—a metal outdoor can that is some twenty years old and filthy. The house is basically unfurnished and I brought with me only my books, my computer, an old stuffed chair and a small table that I was grateful for: I had a table for the lamp I brought. In this house: no side tables, no nothing.

They also left me their car as a gift: It had a flat tire when I arrived and did not have a rearview mirror on the driver's side. It was filthy dirty, with no gas in the tank and a non-working muffler. I couldn't hear if someone beeped; the radio was on but I couldn't hear it except as some sort of odd additional noise and it wouldn't turn off; only the window on the driver's side operated. It cost me 125 bucks to get it in some sort of order so that I could buy a few groceries. I then bought a used car by having the salesman drive to my house with whatever he had—desperate woman gives salesman the 5,000 dollars she's saved in an envelope over eleven years of teaching and hoarding bits of cash (couple hundred bucks for my daughter, slipped in her palm, when she needed it, that sort of money)—and I gave him the car. The second day I drove the car, the air-conditioning died, but the salesman who actually stopped and bought me milk and orange juice when I asked came back and had it fixed (I hoped—it turns out that the air-conditioner had a leak he did *not* fix.) after I had signed the paper releasing him of all warranty and declaring the car I had just bought was a junker—a Missouri law. I am not making this up.

Then I drove to school: The university would not declare me as present and working without showing the strange fiscal officer for the English Department (everyone tells me she is OCD) my actual Social Security card. It did not matter to her that I know my number. She wouldn't accept my passport or driver's license. I had to come back to DC for settlement on the house in Adams Morgan and was able to locate my card, which I obtained when I began working at age 16—you do the math—and no one has ever asked me for. As a result, I will now be paid eventually but I do not have the all-essential employee I.D. number which would allow me to get paid and get an I.D. card and use the library. Perhaps in a few weeks, I will have that number.

And god knows when I will get paid because I appear not to exist.

That is, I fear, a partial story, but here is the good news: I have held up, have only "hit the wall" so to speak once (cried all day the day I had no food, no car, and no way to get food—and that was one week after the initial move). But I love to teach and taught my first class this past Monday, and, as I said, I have a condo in the Penn Quarter (so does D.; it is all very weird, I know) to which I will return as often as I can and permanently in mid-May.

I am writing this on Saturday morning as I wait for the cable guy for whom I waited last week from 8 a.m. to 7 p.m. and who did not show up-no TV reception without cable where I live.

And the professor/writer Marly Swick has befriended me, read my collection and loves it, especially the story "Sine Die," which everyone hates and I think is the best in the series of stories about one woman one day who could no longer cook. Marly has asked me to come speak to both her undergrad and grad writing students the first or second week of classes about that story and my book. I think I've made a true friend. (I did.)

And Missouri is unusually gentle: Yesterday, my mail lady rang my bell—She said, "I have been worried about you—the car was here but the mail was piling up. Are you okay?" I told her I had been briefly away, that I had been having a bit of a hard time here, but that she reassures me about the goodness in the world.

Nietzsche and the Brothers Grimm are not so different. This I am learning. I do wonder if Nietzsche is the reality check on wishes and dreams. I refuse to believe this while I consider the possibility.

She Should Have Known Better

I went to Missouri with a long mane of white hair. Hair and its length in women indicate sexual availability. Think about all the women you've known who cut their hair after they have a child. Oh sure, they say they cut it because they don't have time anymore and there is truth to that assertion: They don't! Or think about religious traditions including mine that require hair to be cut off or covered once a woman has married.

I now see that I knew long before D. left that something in the marriage was amiss because on November 15, 2002, I decided to let my hair grow. I'd worn a buzz cut, a short spiky 'do since I married D. It was wash-and-go, tamed my curly hair and gave me the freedom I *thought* I needed.

I quit my job where I met D. and married him—see the photo, me pencil in hand—and went back to graduate school in 1996.

I never would have quit that job—or now I realize—cut my hair if I'd thought for a minute that he would leave me. He and I made equal salaries, his a bit more than mine even though I was perhaps more successful at my job than he at his. I know what you are thinking: Female emasculates male. She should have known better.

When I let my hair grow, it became wild, frizzy, untamed. D. one morning in the fourth month of this "trial of the hair" took my picture with my hands over my face. I look in that photo like Einstein. I tolerated this untamed hair for what I hoped would come. I despaired but still I hoped. I tried gels and conditioners but nothing worked. I looked like the wild woman of Borneo. I grew up during the age of big rollers and carry-on hood hair driers. What did I know about this hair? What did I know of the meaning of this hair rebellion?

I got off a plane to visit my daughter and her boyfriend, students in graduate school at the University of Chicago, and met my daughter's alarm and unflinching honesty. She pulls no punches: "Your hair looks awful! What are you doing?" And then, her solution in the form of a rhetorical question: "Haven't you ever heard of a curling iron?"

The French Fry Cutter salesman raises his voice on the commercial in my head: "But wait, there's more."

She sat me down on the toilet seat in her tiny bathroom in her miniscule Hyde Park apartment and strand by strand straightened my hair, tamed the hair follicle, lightened its touch to glimmer and shine.

I am too old to look like the goddess that Michelle Obama is, but my hair moved the way hers did that night the prince and princess won the throne: it shone, it "swang" the way Michelle "swings." We all know that she is not tamed. We know that the night Obama won the election men sat in front of their televisions mesmerized by her narrow dress, her delicate hands, her flat stomach and the curve of her hips and all of that started at the top of her head with that 'do.

She "swang" and so did I that night in Chicago. I tossed my hair that, once it had met the curling iron, now lay down in a silver sheen, curled under at the edge of my chin.

I was reborn.

In 1931, the year my mother was nineteen years old, a documentary entitled The Wild Women of Borneo hit the screen. It was black and white, made in the UK. At phrases.org, I find this attempt at definition of the source of the phrase, "[T]his comes from the Victorian circus habit of calling their black show people 'wild' and often attributing their origin to 'Borneo.' They were often displayed wearing only a loin cloth, or similar tropical coverings, wielding a spear, or similar. The crowds were attracted with the call: 'Roll up, roll up, see the wild man of Borneo.' The 'wild man of Borneo' was well established as a concept in the UK before WW2, and possibly earlier. The 'woman' version is merely an extension."

The New York Times tells me this about the film, comment attributed to Hal Erickson:

> To say the least, the title of this 68-minute documentary is misleading. For one thing, we don't see any women until the last few minutes. For another, most of the film was shot in Mexico, which was not then nor is not now anywhere near Borneo. Only after the narrator comments on the natural beauties of the Island of Guadeloupe does the action shift to Borneo, and even then precious few human beings are seen. By the time the 'wild women' show up,

they are so obscured by trees and shrubbery that no one can get a decent look.

When my mother was seventy years old, shortly before her stroke, I was applying her make-up for her birthday. She and I were looking in the mirror at her aged face. She said, "I still see the nineteen-year-old girl."

She was a natural beauty: long dark thick hair, fair skin, hazel eyes, delicate hands. She was obscured by the shrubbery of age. We could both see her through the trees of time. There was no noise while the nineteen year-old girl slid behind the trees.

There was no noise while my hair grew. There was no noise while my daughter tamed the hair follicle with a curling iron.

There was no noise when the avalanche hit in Chamonix, France.

Oz

In Missouri, I fantasize: I am free. I can date. I join JDate, but keep my address as D.C. I can "date" safely? at a distance. I believe in fairy tales.

The prince and princess in the white house have a Portuguese Water dog. The dog's name is Bo because Sasha and Malia's cousins have a cat named Bo and because Mrs. Obama's father was nicknamed Diddley, as in Bo Diddley, who died June 2, 2008. My sister died on that date in 1993, three years after our mother. I wish for them both.

My family has been broken.

The Obama's children are beautiful, perfect and happy. They are the dream. But are they real? Or better: Is what we see real? There is a scrim across their lives. There is a scrim across our view of them.

The Grimm brothers told many stories, some of them barely known. "The Frog-Prince" we all know. And don't we all wish for a time when wishes did some good. Here is the beginning of "Brother and Sister":

> Little brother took his little sister by the hand and said, "Since our mother died we have had no happiness. Our stepmother beats us every day, and if we come near her she kicks us away with her foot. Our meals are hard bread crusts that are leftover and the little dog under the table is better off, for she often throws it a choice morsel.

God pity us. If our mother only knew! Come, we will go forth together
into the wide world."
They walked the whole day over meadows, fields, and stony places.
And when it rained the little sister said, "Heaven and our hearts are
crying together.". . . Then the brother said, "Sister, I am thirsty. If I
knew of a little brook I would go and get a drink. I think I hear one
running." The brother got up and took the little sister by the hand
and they set off to try to find the brook.

My son Ben gave me my wish in December 2006 as I was going on semester break from my visiting writers job at the University of Missouri-Columbia. "Would you like to come to Oz?" he asked.

"Some day, sure," I answer. I don't have a signed separation agreement yet. I am worried about alimony and health care. A vacation? Not possible. I have borrowed money from him to pay my attorney.

D. when he learned this paid Ben back. But the fear revealed by the loan was real even if the fear of D.'s reprisals was not.

Ben bought me a round-trip, business-class ticket to Oz. My son imports and produces serious, ambitious wines from Australia. Before I opened the ticket, he told me not to look at the price. "You are my mother," he said. I did look: 10,000 bucks. I did not have the funds to fly to Australia coach, let alone, the funds to fly in comfort.

I met on this trip almost all the winemakers he imports. I lived for two weeks on his vineyard: wild and craggy, rough-hewn beauty with a view of the sea.

Here's what he said to me when I wasn't on my computer looking for dates with men in D.C.: "You are strong. Don't disappoint me. Move on. It's time. It's way overtime."

I am making dinner at the vineyard one evening and open the refrigerator that is full of wines I cannot afford. I go outside: It is summer in Australia in December when I am there. I ask which white wine I may choose. "Any that suits you," he answers.

And later that night when he is a bit drunk, he howls at me over the fire he has built in the pit on his veranda. The evenings are crisp and cool unlike the heat of the summer day. "I have seen you ask D. for permission too many times. You are free of him. You are free. Don't fucking ever ask again for permission to drink a wine in my house. Do you understand me? You are free now. Be strong. Choose, woman!"

In the morning, he asks if he has been cruel. I reassure that he has not. "Good advice," I say and we move on—though my heart still breaks for D.

Ben and I part at the airport in Adelaide with tears withheld but visible inside his eyes. I think of the way a lake holds back the sea's surge as a storm pushes its force from afar. He puts on his shades. I get on the plane.

Ben is not speaking to D. (a great difficulty for me who has two children. I talked to both of them too much and inappropriately when D. left me. They are not in full agreement on this point. I suspect my daughter has worked out this trouble with me to some extent but not fully. They both feel "jerked around," as Ben has put it. And rightly so. Who was I, their mother, to turn to them like the weepy school girl?)

This difficulty, somewhat shared by the two, should not be placed in a parentheses but there I place it with this from E. E. Cummings' poem that begins,

> since feeling is first . . .

and that ends:

> we are for each other: then
>
> laugh, leaning back in my arms
>
> for life's not a paragraph
>
> And death i think is no parenthesis

What my son does not know is that the return flight was the beginning of my virtual dating and my fantasies about sex after sixty. What he does not know is that what happened on the flight from San Francisco to D.C. could never have happened if I had flown in coach.

My flight was delayed five hours in San Francisco, so long that the crew changed while most of us stayed on the plane, thinking it would take off soon. It did not. I had already been traveling some twenty or more hours to get from Adelaide to Sydney and Sydney to San Francisco and to the plane that would take me home. I was jet-lagged and I slept through the five-hour delay. Before I fell asleep, I saw a tall, slim elegant older man, a young seventy was my guess, wearing a blue suede sport jacket—strikingly beautiful and an unusual choice for what looked to me like a forceful man. He walked the aisles and flipped open his cell phone with purpose—determined I suspected to get another flight.

The CEO.

I sleep and write down this dream when I wake:

I have been watching a college baseball game. Men are playing. Ryan, my son-in-law, is hitting and fielding and I am wondering why he would choose this school when he could have gone somewhere so much better (of course I wake to remember that he played baseball at Dartmouth) but in the dream he attends a no-name school I also attend. There is a point in the game where I can see the ball coming, know just where it should be struck and have the desire to enter the field, to pick up the bat, to hit it so that the wood cracks with the precision of a well-hit ball, with the sound of wood against leather that is the right-spot sound. The bat does not break.

Then I am crossing the street, leaving the field and the wind is blowing so hard against me that I can see myself as the arc of the letter C trying to cross the street. Someone says, "She may be blown away, she's light, a feather against it," but I hold true. I am wearing a pale taupe coat like the coats Audrey Hepburn wore in Charade. I am wearing low heels, pumps like hers. I make it across the street. I make it through the wind. I make it.

How absurd: old woman dreams herself young, like her beautiful daughter who is married to Ryan: my daughter Sarah, the knock-out with brains.

When I woke, I took my quart bag (post 9-11: all liquids must fit in such a bag) and walked toward the restroom to try to repair my face and the CEO met me in the space between the door and the flight attendant station: the galley. I went into the restroom, rattled by the fact that he had made eye-contact with me. He was standing there when I came out, by the way without my quart bag and it was never to be found. He handed me a slip of paper with his e-mail address on it and these words, "Looking is an over-rated feminine attribute." But I had misread the note. I later learned that he had written "Cooking" instead of "Looking." He talked to me briefly; I had been chatting with the woman and her husband behind me; she had been out in the airport and bought some wine she'd shared with him. I had told her something about my book. He and she had talked.

I was too rattled to recall what he said to me in the galley or on the Dulles transport that took us to baggage claim.

When home and after a good long sleep, I wrote him a note with my e-mail address and quoted his line about "looking."

He replied:

Dear Mary,

Just back a few hours ago from D.C. and still a bit punchy from the flight, accumulated mail, etc.

The napkin your "fellow traveler" gave me had your name and as I recall, a line about your book. My scrawled note was intended to say "Cooking is an over-rated feminine attribute," meant in jest of course in reaction to *The Woman Who Never Cooked*. Your themes struck me as a fascinating combination that I'd not ordinarily (perhaps never) associate. Fascinating, to the extent I'd like to know how you connected them. I'll order a copy tomorrow.

I enjoyed our ultra-brief intersection.

From the opposite coast (Saratoga CA).

And signed with his full name (he is highly googleable). Here he shall be lower-case d.

And I replied with this babble:

Dear d.,

And, me, after actually some thirty-four hours traveling from Australia, at that point wearing no make-up and carrying around that mass of curly hair that I usually wear more elegantly. Well, here's what happened to me after you actually spoke to me: I lost my quart bag (that security requirement for lipstick, etc.), because I became flustered—more below on this state of mind. The quart bag had in it my perfume (Opium, by the way) and other quite expensive little bits of female trivia, considered essential by this female to cover the flaws. No steward could then find the little bag. The super pretty one who looked like Nicole Kidman and was quite aware of our bit of intrigue—had an observant eye, apparently—tried her best to help me find it but failed. I was thus unable to do any repair work—so you have seen the bare truth of the matter.

I am now about to sound like a character out of a Victorian novel here—but what happened is that I "swooned" when you came over to me in the galley—or in today's vernacular, lost my cool, assuming I ever had any of that.

Mary

His next subject line is: Can this be???

Dear Mary,

I've ordered *The Woman Who Never Cooked* and look forward to it, wondering the extent to which it was shaped by personal experience, the experiences of others you knew and/or a vivid imagination. All three? I paint watercolors to exercise the right brain, but I've long felt that "writing" (especially fiction) ranks at the top of creative endeavors.

I confess to no little amazement about our "instant connection" since objectively we've interacted in person for exactly 47 seconds. Even with our e-mails it has been ultra-brief. (With glances, etc., it becomes more reasonable wouldn't you say?) As a writer you must have something to say about the chemistry of spontaneous mutual personal attraction, no?

Your description of your bag of feminine accoutrements provoked smiles and may I remind you that my remark when you said something about not being at your best was along the lines of: "You cannot hide good looks," something I believe. Naturally it was also intended to put you at ease. Good looks and intellect are a marvelous combination!

In the spirit of full disclosure, I was on my way to spend New Year's eve with a woman I met on a cruise last year. After what seems like endless months of dealing with loss, I impulsively signed onto a cruise aboard a small ship and made a new friend. I seem to be on an uncertain path, ping-ponging between monasticism and tentative engagement. Best I stop here, lest I tell you more than you'd like.

When I've read your book, I'd like to confer, knowing in advance that it will be stimulating, thought-provoking and perhaps a glimpse of MLT beyond that on UAL 782.

d.

And he does read my book, and he does write again. And once again I swoon:

Dear Sleeping Beauty,

"Sleeping Beauty" is as I first remember you in Seat 7C across two aisles, supine and lovely. The last indelible image is of you turning away with your luggage in tow at Dulles to connect with your driver to take you home in Washington. Your departure seemed abrupt and yet I didn't know how it could have been otherwise at that stage.

I refuse to say how many times I looked across the aisle, somewhat amazed that you were engaged in animated conversation with the young woman sitting next. (You must have been running on pure adrenalin.). Had you two been in opposite seats you'd have been aware of my glances, so perhaps just as well.

Funny thought as I hiked local hills this afternoon: What do you suppose might have transpired had we been in adjacent seats on 782? My guess is that at some point a cabin attendant might have suggested "more decorum" to put it politely.

d.

It is three years later and I have not met him. We corresponded via e-mail for two of those years and he called me two or three times this past year—the last time, I did not answer and he did not leave a message. At one point, the woman in Washington fell quite ill, a brain tumor and lung cancer. He told me about her trials. I hoped she'd recover. I viewed him loyal and true to her.

I value loyalty as does my son. But unlike my son, I value imperfection.

Virtual dating had begun. My son had made it possible. Wishing had begun.

I dreamed of a large wave that rises in the sea. I see it coming, don't know what to do but hold an inside rail along the wall of the boat. The wave rides large and full and I float with it, my head barely above it, still holding on. And it does not break. It rides over the entire boat and, in the dream, out to sea, though this is not possible as we are at harbor. If this were not a dream, the wave would have hit the shore, but it did not. The sea was before and behind us. Behind me.

That was the wish.

Here are the worries: I worry about what I did to my children. I have two children who went through a hard time with me after D. "needed to be alone" and all the wreckage that came with that decision. They both heard things from a mother that even grown children, both over thirty, should not have heard: I spoke hard and sad about D. I did not know what I was doing. I worried them. I was weak and broken. I was romantic, silly, and searching.

I worry about two strikes—Yes, this is my second marriage that has broken.

I am learning about repair.

But I also know what wishing can do. In the grim Grimm story, the sister knows that if her brother drinks from the spring, he will become bewitched. She saves him from the fate of becoming a tiger who would tear her to pieces and of becoming a wolf who would eat her. She cannot save him from the fate of drinking finally from the brook that will turn him into a young roebuck.

Instead, here is what she does:

Now the sister cried over her poor bewitched brother, and the little roe wept also, sitting sorrowfully near to her.
But at last the girl said, "Be quiet, dear little roe. I will never, never leave you."

Then she untied her golden garter and put it around the roebuck's neck, and she plucked rushes and wove them into a soft cord. This she tied to the little animal and led it on, walking deeper and deeper into the forest.

And when they had gone a very long way they came at last to a little house, and the girl looked in, and as it was empty, she thought, "We can stay here and live." Then she sought for leaves and moss to make a soft bed for the roe, and every morning she went out and gathered roots and berries, and nuts for herself, and brought tender grass for the roe, who ate out of her hand, and was content and played round her. In the evening, when the sister was tired and had said her prayer, she laid her head on the roe's back: that was her pillow, and she slept softly on it. And if only the brother had had his human form, it would have been a delightful life.

Or, I ask, would it? For do we really know what wish has been fulfilled?

Let the Rom-Coms Roll

I turn to the Rom-Com for answers. Don't be quick to discount: Wisdom comes where you look.

I have watched *Hitch* more times than I can count. I'm obsessed with this movie and many others—*Four Weddings and a Funeral*, for another (You don't want to know how many times I have watched and wept over that one.)

Here's how the best ones work: *Hitch*, the first example: Two cynics meet, neither believes love works, one or both have been hurt or screwed by believing that the open heart is a good thing. So one, or in this case both, have closed off that option: closed heart, closed heart.

Open heart, open heart lying behind the little box we carry in our chests. Who's got the key to the box?

I think, LOVE? Doesn't exist. I've got the key to my box. I can shoot hoops (double entendre: look it up) while I wait, but I can look and look I do.

On JDate I meet m., real-estate developer. I come home from Oz to my condo with all its boxes to meet him. He's my age, a bit overweight, a widower, who reminds me of D. Not the body—D.'s body, slim and hard and tight—but m.'s height, the blue eyes, the open face draw me. He has two teenage girls, a newly built house he and his wife had bought and designed before she fell ill with a pernicious form of breast cancer. She died three months after diagnosis.

We meet at Oya in downtown D.C. near my condo, and we have dinner at a hard-to-get good table he has finagled. He orders good wine and we both order good au courant Asian-French tapas. We talk about grief. I tell about the losses of my mother, my sister, three years apart, and then the loss of my father, slowly. All the deaths were slow and painful, my mother and sister over my youth and adulthood and my father over the ten years I was finally doing what I had waited my whole life to do, as Elisabeth Bishop says in "One Art,"

> . . . the art of losing's not too hard to master though it may look
> like (*Write* it!) like disaster.

m. comes back to my condo and we talk sitting on my pale white leather wrap-around couch. He tells me that, after his wife died, he quit his job to take care of his girls, works as a consultant so that he has flexible hours. He tells me he bought in Paris a Sean Sculley painting I love and have seen at The Phillips Gallery. He had bought it before Sculley hit hot in the U.S. He met Sculley's agent in Paris and then reneged on the deal with the good-hearted agent who understood m. needed the money back—some one-hundred-thousand dollars for a painting that is now worth six times that—to take care of his girls. He tells me he'd been a bit reckless when he bought the art he still adores and has lost.

m. is looking for a job as his girls find their way through grief that comes on them like tidal waves he can't handle. But he has a shrink and she is helping him find his way. He is not in typical mourning because what his girls may or may not know is that he and his wife were about to separate before she fell ill, that they were wending their way toward what would have probably been the result of the counseling they were joined in. He married late. He screwed around, many short-term relationships before he finally married. He tells me he understands now that he has trouble with commitment, that he has trouble with intimacy, that his childhood laid the foundation, as all our childhoods make us who we are. He tells me that we must find our own way through to discover who we are to become.

A lot revealed on a first date and we wrap around each other in understanding. I am not good at being the cynic and tell him about the loss of D. He listens. He is quiet and reserved but full of heart—and reckless for art.

He asks, "Do I need to take care of you?" He has come over in the afternoon the day after the first date. He tells me he has a girlfriend, but that relationship is ending. He wants to make love. So do I, I think. He's one of the good guys, I think (and still do.)

I have the key to my box. I can do this. "I can take care of myself," I answer, and we make love.

He comes over the next afternoon. He is tired. We lie down on my bed, clothed, and we both sleep—relaxed, safe, intimate.

And then I go to Williamstown to visit my daughter and son-in-law for New Year's. I have told Sarah and her husband Ryan about m. Before I board the plane, I sit at BWI and talk to m. on the phone before he is to be interviewed by the boarding school, very near Williamstown, where his oldest daughter hopes to go to prep school. I give advice about what he should say: Open heart, be concrete, I say from my cell phone to his: He'd called *me*.

Ryan meets me at the Albany airport. When Ryan sees me he says I am flushed. "Did you do it with m.?" he asks. I demur, and Ryan knows. Sarah and Ryan look at his profile on JDate. He is not Jewish but likes Jewish women. His wife was Jewish. Sarah cooks a gourmet dinner and we go to the Williamstown Theater to see the only thing playing, *Holiday*, writer-director Nancy Myers (*Something's Gotta Give*—my daughter and I saw that one together in New York—and *Baby Boom* that Myers did when she was still married to her partner). Sarah says about Jude Law and Cameron Diaz, "This is going to happen to you, is happening. I want this for you. I want you happy again. Maybe he's the one." Sarah loves the Rom-Coms, too.

Sarah, after all was said and done with m., and more tries that came after (yes, I will tell), doesn't think I write the story I'm telling you with enough irony. She thinks I am sentimental. "You need to be more ironized," she advises. I think, Is that really a word? as I see myself on the board and the iron of life rolling over me. I think of all the ways that life betrays the living. I think of Tillie Olsen, "I Stand Here Ironing," the short story in *Tell Me a Riddle*. Tell me a riddle, please.

m. doesn't call. I return to D.C. and then late in January to Missouri to finish out the second semester of my visiting writer job. I wait like a school-girl for the phone to ring. And finally, after more than a month, I send an e-mail: How are you? I ask. He replies, and signs his, "Warm regards."

And then one night about another month later, he calls me at 11:30 at night and explains that he had trouble finding my number. He accuses me of being cool when I answer (not in the sense we meant that word when we were young in the fifties and still believed in love—or thought we did). He woke me. I am not good near midnight. Too much hope.

Too much Cinderella: The Grimm Brothers tell us, *Cinderella had jumped quickly down from the back of the pigeon house* (where she had been hiding after she had danced with and escaped from the prince) *and had run to the little hazel-tree, and there she had taken off her beautiful clothes and laid them on her mother's grave.*

I write this e-mail:

> Dear m.,
>
> I have hidden my profile on JDate. I have needed time to think about what I am about in all this, how much I need to be loved sincerely and wholly. And I need to search for that with the knowledge that passionate, joyous intimate love is rare and hard to find.
>
> I did not mean to be cool last night, but I was quite tired. And I did not know how to express what I am saying here without appearing to blame you. I do not blame you. I did what I did with you because I wanted to. I do think now that I was reckless. That is what you were hearing last night when I made the comment about the lateness of your call.
>
> I am glad that you called. But I do think that it is probably no accident that my number was not in your address book. I was not on your center stage, so to speak. You were on mine for a brief and lovely respite in my life.
>
> Whether or not we might recapture that is to be seen.
>
> Best,
>
> Mary

PS: I sign my note "best" and you signed yours "warm regards." One must wonder if I did indeed have the "zipless fuck" with you. I don't think that's what happened. But it is how it felt in the aftermath.

He calls in the morning and tells me he has met a woman in New York and that he thinks this one is for real.

You've got to admire the honesty.

And the break in my heart that is not his fault, widened. But I *was* ironized. That's a good thing, isn't it?

I find this on the Internet:

HOW DO YOU DECIDE WHO TO MARRY? (written by kids)

You got to find somebody who likes the same stuff. Like, if you like sports, she should like it that you like sports, and she should keep the chips and dip coming. -- Alan, age 10

No person really decides before they grow up who they're going to marry. God decides it all way before, and you get to find out later who you're stuck with. -- Kristen, age 10

WHAT IS THE RIGHT AGE TO GET MARRIED?

Twenty-three is the best age because you know the person FOREVER by then. -- Camille, age 10

HOW CAN A STRANGER TELL IF TWO PEOPLE ARE MARRIED?

You might have to guess, based on whether they seem to be yelling at the same kids. -- Derrick, age 8

WHAT DO YOU THINK YOUR MOM AND DAD HAVE IN COMMON?

Both don't want any more kids. -- Lori, age 8

WHAT DO MOST PEOPLE DO ON A DATE?

Dates are for having fun, and people should use them to get to know each other. Even boys have something to say if you listen long enough. -- Lynnette, age 8 (isn't she a treasure?)

On the first date, they just tell each other lies and that usually gets them interested enough to go for a second date. -- Martin, age 10

WHAT WOULD YOU DO ON A FIRST DATE THAT WAS TURNING SOUR?

I'd run home and play dead. The next day I would call all the newspapers and make sure they wrote about me in all the dead columns. -- Craig, age 9

WHEN IS IT OKAY TO KISS SOMEONE?

When they're rich. -- Pam, age 7

The law says you have to be eighteen, so I wouldn't want to mess with that. -- Curt, age 7

The rule goes like this: If you kiss someone, then you should marry them and have kids with them. It's the right thing to do. -- Howard, age 8

IS IT BETTER TO BE SINGLE OR MARRIED?

It's better for girls to be single but not for boys. Boys need someone to clean up after them.-- Anita, age 9 (Bless you child.)

HOW WOULD THE WORLD BE DIFFERENT IF PEOPLE DIDN'T GET MARRIED?

There sure would be a lot of kids to explain, wouldn't there? -- Kelvin, age 8

And the #1 Favorite is:

HOW WOULD YOU MAKE A MARRIAGE WORK?

Tell your wife that she looks pretty, even if she looks like a truck. -- Ricky age 10

These children are too young for the Rom-Com. Most of these films are rated R because of partial nudity: Sex is a key part of romance and of comedy. I ask, What is the most ridiculous position two people get in? Think about how it looks, not in the movies but, horrors, from a mirror in the ceiling.

In *Hitch*, as in most good romantic comedies—after all they *are* comedies— a misperception or unfortunate coincidence takes over the film before one or both cynics can see LOVE for what it might actually be: inexorable, indomitable, irrefutable, life-changing.

One could argue that coincidence drives the ending of *Romeo and Juliet*. I argue that the world of propriety could not bear their love.

Read any love stories in the news lately? Except for Michelle and Barack?

Love, actually: (Also another Rom-Com) Does it exist? Or do we all need to be ironized?

Like a Coin

A story I made up while sleeping: a woman, dark-haired—like me when I was young—with a man, a stocky, hairy man who takes my hand. We walk along the water. I don't know where we are. He takes me into a rehearsal hall. Now we are on Coney Island at the Yiddish Russian restaurant there. The boardwalk is cold and windy. It is winter. We eat borscht and peroshki, shots of vodka. We are tired from the windy walk, from the vodka shots. He takes me to a room with a bed and we lie down, not to make love but to rest. He takes off his shirt and pants because they are cold, damp from the sea air. We get under the covers and I lay my head on his hairy chest.

D., aka the husband, has a hairless chest with a swatch of now grey hair where the sternum makes its dip between his pecs. I find this man comfortable and sleep, my legs wrapped around one of his.

I no longer know the meaning of betrayal. It is like a coin, two-sided.

First Kiss

I must find the way through all the screens on the stage that slide one in front of the other. I want to shout, "Fire." Like the clown in the theatre who called out to the laughing crowd while the coulisses burned, while the crowd applauded, disbelieving. I slide the scenery panels of my life through the backstage grooves while they burn and no one sees the fire.

In *Charade*, when Reggie/Audrey says to Sylvie, "I admit I came to Paris to escape American traditional, but that doesn't mean I'm ready for French Provincial," she has just told Sylvie she is going to get a divorce because she does not love Charles. "That's no reason to get a divorce," Sylvie counters. "With this years' clothes . . ." On that mountain in the Alps, Reggie has no idea where Charles is.

I had no idea where or who D. was.

Do you remember when Michelle Obama wowed Paris shortly after Barack took office, when she kissed Sarkozy while Barack tried to figure out the 'bise' with both Carla Bruni and a young girl in a crowd? Barack demurred I read in Britain's *The Daily Mail*: "Mr. Obama . . . apparently pointed out that his wife, Michelle, was watching." Finally Sarkozy persuaded him to allow himself to receive the traditional French greeting.

And didn't we all wonder what Carla and Michelle had for lunch? Or am I the only one, a thin woman, with an obsession over what everyone is eating and who is cooking?

D. had no problem with the kissing of other women in front of me—I who cooked like a mad woman in search of the perfect recipe, in search of the joining of family, in search of the belovéd. I'd heard him sigh after I'd made angel hair pasta with pesto, after I'd roasted the chicken with caramelized carrots and onions, after I'd placed in front of him my first fork-stirred omelet lightly dusted with white cheddar cheese before I'd rolled it onto his plate.

Two years before we separated, D. kissed the first woman at Cloud in Dupont Circle, at the bar. I walked home alone at half past midnight, a lipstick in my pocket (no keys, no money) and waited for them, D. and S., a woman I had begun chatting with at Firefly down the street on New Hampshire Avenue. We had been eating dinner at the bar.

Firefly: In the dusk and then the dark, fireflies flash their tails. Male fireflies control this flash of light to signal their desire; females flash their willingness. It's a cold light, no heat, the result of a chemical inside them: Luciferin. Their taste to predators is bitter. Some say that frogs who eat too many of them may also glow. I've wondered how the frogs consume the bitter taste. Why aren't they warned off with the first bite?

I watched them, D. and S., with a bitter taste in my mouth.

I walked home and waited for them on the stoop of our four-story one-hundred-year-old Victorian that we were renovating in Adams Morgan. Actually, D. renovated the old lady, relentlessly, for seven years. I wanted all the men out of my house so that I could write: I worked in the fourth floor attic. That night I ended up putting S. to bed in the third floor guest room. When the two finally left Cloud, S. was smashed. Her Mercedes was parked somewhere in a garage nearby. A homeless man helped D. get her into a cab after she fell, hit her chin on the curb. I learned, as I cared for her with an ice bag and a cup of Chamomile tea, that she had just had a facelift and the bleeding on her chin was a slit in the work of the artist: the plastic surgeon.

In the morning, I met them at the long granite island in my chef's kitchen. D. had made S. a cappuccino from our Miele built-into-the-wall espresso machine.

You're thinking? It was quite a kitchen. Okay so maybe you're not thinking that but you must know that this kitchen had a place for everything and everything in its place. This part of the renovation I had a hand in. Thus, my obsession with the refrigerator and its metaphor: I'm getting to that. But for now: Get this: I had three SubZeros: the refrigerator and freezer and the two refrigerator drawers in the island for fresh fruits and vegetables and meat and fish.

I ask the two: "So you want to tell me what was going on last night?"

S. looks truly bemused. D. does not. I tell them that they were— Well, you get the picture. D. has nothing to say. S. tells me—and I believe her—that she doesn't remember, that she doesn't know D. from anywhere except last night, that she's divorced with one child and that if we could take her home, she'd be most grateful. We do: I vomit in her bathroom. I am overwhelmed with loss and throwing up my food seems the exact right response. I think this after I clean her toilet, wipe her sink and beg to be returned to our Old Lady of a house.

When we are home, D. gives the explanation that turns out later to actually make quite a bit of sense even if it did not at the time: "I don't know what I am doing."

You've got to admire this kind of honesty. Have I said that before?

After all, I love him. After all, he loves me. After all, we are all flawed human beings. After all, we are all in search of the belovéd.

Later, I focused on what Michelle and Barack might be having for dinner in Paris and Barack's confrontation with 'the bise.'

The only doughs I haven't made are puff pastry and brioche. When I wrote this line, I wondered if it should have been the first line of this story. But clearly it was not as I had then become the woman who never cooked.

Here's a Talmudic question I have puzzled over—the one about the two men in the desert. Only one has water. If he shares it, they both die; if he keeps it, he lives and his companion dies. What should he do? Rabbi Akiva taught that the man should drink it. And so I considered after D. left me if I should cook anymore. After all, my mother died in 1990, my sister three years later at 53, and my father hard on her heels.

And then D. kissed S.

And then and then and then. Bad transition.

On that day after the night of the kiss, I no longer believed I would cook.

I did believe in *The Princess and the Frog*. My hair is shoulder length—and snow white. I am no virgin princess, but I sure want the fairy tale. I want to go to sleep and be awakened by my prince.

But how do we know who is who? We are in the game of Charades.

Deceptive Cadence

My husband used to play the console piano we owned only for me—never for anyone else. Before he left me, he bought a 17,000-dollar-black baby grand and placed this Kawai in the front parlor of our old Victorian brownstone before we sold it.

This piano now graces his condo where he lives alone.

I had wanted to buy him a new piano for the last decade: a gift for his birthday. With his perfect pitch and sense of touch, I needed him to play the piano I would buy him but he refused to touch a keyboard in a store.

On the old console that he, with his perfect pitch, refused to get tuned the last years we lived in the house . . .

The houses are all gone under the sea.

. . . on this piano, whose notes must have jarred his ears, he played Shubert's Opus 90, No. 3 in G Flat. He played it from the old yellow Schirmer's Library Classics, Four Impromptus book that his mother had bought him. His name in her script in pencil is still on the cover as if he were just another of her many students. A note in ink on the front says Andante Mosso, G with the flat mark in her handwriting and on the table of contents a note that says "prelude" next to the number 3. She was planning to play it for church, prelude to the service. She had written in pencil on page twenty-one of the book whose pages have all come apart: "9 to 10 minutes." Rubenstein plays this piece in about six and a quarter minutes. She used to tell her son, "If you're having trouble, slow down." She took her own advice.

Mosso means literally "motion." I want to know that he is moved. I won't be able to hear the piano, but, from having listened—since he has gone—from listening endlessly to Rubenstein on a recording, I know it's the melody that will move him. He has told me that the melody is exceedingly simple, that any child could play it (I don't believe this), but this I do know: The melody rings only if all the other keys are struck well and swiftly. It's these complicated patterns that make you wonder how it's done, think there's more going on than two hands could possibly do, when you hear Horowitz or Rubenstein do it—when I have heard *him* do it. I imagine that when he played it as a boy at the piano that lay against the wall of his childhood parlor, from the kitchen his mother would say, "Now I can hear the melody," as he tried to get those eighth notes rolling properly, playing up and down the chords, repeatedly, taking the chords and breaking them into their parts, fluidly and separately. Success at this gives the piece its complexity, assures that the rapid notes don't overwhelm the melody, that both are heard as separate and integrated strands.

I wish for a window near his that I could open and listen: He begins the piece, rolls the eighth notes in his right hand, lightly letting the whole notes ring in his left hand, tries ever so hard to play the whole notes and half notes and quarter notes with that ringing, bell-like tone his mother hoped for.

I once told him a story about dance, an old rabbi's tale: a story of the deaf who see the sound and join the dance.

We were deaf, could see the sound, but had no dance.

He touched me the way he touched the keys of the piano. A practiced touch to hold my center, to touch my string that lies on my soundboard, to raise my pitch. He wasn't erect when he touched me. Did he love me? I resisted the letting go though he was always able to get to me, finally, if he played my keys, played them long enough, varied his touch, reassured me that I would come. But I resisted because often he couldn't enter after. I now know he *was* aroused.

He couldn't explain and, cruelly, I accused.

The writer lives in shame of what she's done and what she tells.

I had to be beneath him for him to come, had to support him with my hand for him to enter. Such an easy thing to do. Such an intimate thing to do.

And yet when he finally left me, I hoped he'd imagine me with another man who, when I lay on my side, would touch me, arousing me in a new way, in a way I hadn't known possible.

I want him to imagine this man above me, his head flushed, his eyes on me, my hands around his head, my muscles still flexing because I had not come to climax. I could not go fully with any man but my husband.

And then I was sure I would not have him again.

> *The dancers are all gone under the hill.*

He rolls into the G flat major bars, as he deepens his touch in the left hand, the single note melody rising from the strings and the soundboard and then at the same time moving up and down softly on the keys that are the background in the piece. He won't falter as the piece softens and slows to its first quiet dying fall because he will know through the playing that I have understood that to climax will be the ultimate betrayal of him.

He won't finish the Schubert: this man with perfect pitch. He will take his hands from the keys, place them in his lap and listen because the music vibrates in our ears when the sound is gone if we will only listen, not move on to something else, but listen, we who have been deaf.

He won't complete the piece. Each time he comes to the penultimate page, page twenty-seven, there will be his mother's words on the third staff where the quarter notes are marked *crescendo* and where below the c whole note that is held for a two-quarter count followed by the d-flat, held for one-quarter, are her words in pencil that refer to the eighth notes in the right hand, *deceptive cadence*, and his hands will not move forward.

> *The houses are all gone under the sea.*
>
> *The dancers are all gone under the hill*

Catch a Falling Star

I have a note on the poem "Song," quoting my professor Andrew Bongiorno (1900-98) at Oberlin where I got my first master's degree and where I met Tom: "cynical poem although jaunty and vigorous" (or perhaps this is my note as it is not in red pencil, the color I used during class, but I don't speak this way). Therefore it must be Bongiorno. Bongiorno, I learned long after I worshipped him, began teaching without the PhD he later earned. He would never be hired now by Oberlin where he remains revered. I learn of the PhD elsewhere (Cornell, 1935). Here's what I read after Bongiorno had died, written by his godchild Andrew Ward who tells of urging Bongiorno to accept an honorary degree, "I told him that he owed it not only to himself and the students who revered him, but to the endangered vocation of teaching itself. It would at least throw a wrench into the new Oberlin that would never have hired Andrew, let alone given him tenure, because he tended to teach rather than publish and lacked a PhD."

Bongiorno taught me that "we must be literal-minded because no poem can be completely our own as long as we are ignorant or even uncertain of the denotation of a single word in any line, of a single common or proper noun."

Answer true or false. This imperative serves facts such as, Pluto is a planet. Oh, once good, no longer good. Answer true or false: D. has betrayed.

I refuse to answer.

Here is the poem by John Donne,

> Song
>
> Go and catch a falling star,
>
> Get with child a mandrake root,
>
> Tell me where all past years are,
>
> Or who cleft the devil's foot,
>
> Teach me to hear mermaids singing,
>
> Or to keep off envy's stinging,
>
>> And find
>>
>> What wind
>
> Serves to advance an honest mind.
>
> If thou be'st born to strange sights.
>
> Things invisible to see,
>
> Ride ten thousand days and nights,
>
> Till age snow white hairs on thee,
>
> Thou, when thou return'st, wilt tell me
>
> All strange wonders that befell thee,
>
>> And swear
>>
>> Nowhere
>
> Lives a woman true and fair.
>
> If thou find'st one, let me know;
>
> Such a pilgimage were sweet.
>
> Yet do not; I would not go,
>
> Though at next door we might meet.
>
> Though she were true when you met her,
>
> And last till you write your letter,
>
>> Yet she will
>>
>> Will be
>
> False, ere I come, to two or three.

I spent more nights than I can count in the library with the Oxford English Dictionary—that I now own—to read the poems Bongiorno assigned, to find the meaning of a word in the year Donne wrote it. At the side of the OED I fell in love with a man named Tom who was in my class. I can no longer recall his last name.

Parapraxes?

Here is what happened: We attended Bongiorno's class. We went to lunch together. We studied together in the library, passing the OED to one another.

I lived in the Quadrangle because I was a graduate student and had an apartment there. He came back with me and we lay on the floor, making out, coming close to sex. I was a virgin. He did not know this. (I turned twenty-one; Tom took me off-campus—Oberlin was dry in the '60s—for my first drink: an apricot brandy sour). He refused to go further than the kissing and touching and clinging, a restraint that strikes me now as romantic and erotic like a good dream.

One night when I was alone in my apartment: A knock on the door. This was the sound of the inevitable: A woman stood before me. She said, "I am engaged to Tom _____."

The Bongiorno class was over. I never saw Tom again. I wept. I ached. I suppose he married her. After all, he was Catholic and I, Jewish. Verbotten in the first place.

I loved Andrew Bongiorno's class and have never forgotten his name. I loved Tom and have forgotten his surname.

My first husband danced with his secretary all night at a Christmas party while her husband and I watched. Some six months before he had told me at a lunch in a noisy restaurant near his office that he had been dreaming of her. Her name was Mary. I am not making this up. While I was crying, he had a side-table meeting with a business associate. He later told me that he had done much more with Mary than see her in his sleep. I asked, "Why are you telling me?" He answered, "Because it's over." Six months later when he ordered the tent and camping equipment for her for Christmas, when I was buying his other two secretaries their gifts: small vases or whatnots under thirty bucks, I asked for an explanation. He confessed. I tried to forget.

No parapraxes on this one.

He had built me a house with the kitchen of my dreams that my mother helped design and he kept the house when we divorced: Non-negotiable. I did not have it appraised. He told me what it was worth. He did not marry his secretary, but he did remarry: a lovely woman I now am quite fond of.

Could I have guessed that my second husband would build me a chef's kitchen and then kiss two women over two years in front of me?

While my second new kitchen was being built I went to the hospital for a knee repair.

On the day of the surgery at Sibley Hospital in D.C. not far from the old house with its four stories and the empty kitchen that D. and I were renovating, I went to sleep. No one dreams under general anesthesia. Out cold. But if I had dreamt, I would have dreamt of j., the man I met on the number five bus. That was after I'd left my first brand new kitchen—before the electrician had hooked up the new GE oven, built-in microwave under the hood—*and* my first husband who'd been having the affair.

I left this man I'd called "my husband" for the last ten years and who now seemed like anything but. I couldn't even say his name out loud anymore. He'd become a nameless fixture in my life and in the house he'd built for us with a big wide kitchen, almost finished, with brand new fixtures for everything, many of which I also couldn't name. I'd picked out knobs and buttons and switches and faucets, all with names and order numbers that had to be remembered or who knows what would have happened?

That new house was like none I'd ever seen or ever hoped for. In the kitchen, the trash can was hidden behind a cabinet and conveniently tipped forward when I pulled on the door. I had a hidden ironing board. Not that that had much to do with cooking, but the laundry room was right off the mud room, off the kitchen, near the back stairway. A back stairway! That new kitchen had a fireplace too and the all-important suburban deck.

I grew up in a Baltimore row house with stairs to the second floor and stairs to the basement and a view from the front door to the back door and the clothes tree outside the door. My childhood house didn't have hallways or a foyer. There was no place to hide anything or to hide. I could hear the neighbors when they argued and everything that everyone said inside my narrow house was fair game for anyone in the back, the front, up or down the stairs.

After I left my first husband, I lived with my two children in a tiny house about the size of the kitchen in the new house he'd built and insisted was *his*. And I began riding the number five bus to the job I'd found in downtown D.C.

On that bus I met j. I'd been looking at him for weeks and didn't know if he'd been looking at me because it seemed that everyone was looking at me when I dragged my three bags onto the bus each morning—my briefcase, my purse, my gym bag—and invariably dropped one of them. One morning, he retrieved my purse, handed it to me. And I met his eyes, so brown, so intense that in that brief moment of eye contact I felt as if I were traveling so fast I might die. I'd heard that if you could travel at the speed of light, you'd become light itself. Like matter changing into energy. I could barely look at him.

One day, standing at the subway after the bus ride, he'd spoken to me and somehow I'd given him my first name and apparently enough information to find me at my job because that's exactly what he did. He called and asked me to lunch. I was seduced by the force of his effort.

At lunch, I had even more trouble looking at him, trouble not touching his long thin fingers, the silver rope bracelet on his wrist. I did slip one finger beneath the bracelet on parting and to my horror nearly swooned like an ingénue in a Victorian novel.

He calls. He pursues.

After I sleep with him at lunchtime at the Tabard Inn on N street, against my better judgment and with an unrestrained excitement I'd never known and would never know again, I also learn that he is married.

I would have dreamt all this because kitchens and men and new men and old ones and getting old and needing repair, and Viking stoves, and big-chested refrigerators are all about love despite what your stomach tells you. I knew this the way I knew that my kitchen was going, going, gone because I think somewhere deep down I knew that D. didn't love me anymore.

From "Indifferent," by John Donne. Read *indifferent* here as the OED suggests at the date of this poem as *impartial*.

> *Will no other vice content you?*
>
> *Will it not serve your turn to do as your mothers?*
>
> *Or have you all old vices spent, and now would find out*
> *others?*
>
> *Or doth a fear that men are true torment you?*
>
> *Oh, we are not; be not you so;*
>
> *Let me, and do you, twenty know.*
>
> *Rob me, but bind me not, and let me go.*

Bongiorno continues to advise, "The search for literal meanings need not be regarded as a necessary evil. Its aim is the discovery of a large part of the poem's significance, and the lover of poetry must overcome every tendency to find it irksome. The teacher who recognizes the value of this literal-mindedness not only will teach the student how to read a lyric, but will teach him, at least implicitly, that the rational and the imaginative are not contraries but complements, that the loftiest, no less the humblest, productions of the human spirit owe their being to man's reason as well as to his imagination."

Answer true or false:

Betrayal equals Mary.

Mary equals betrayal.

Therefore, Mary has not been betrayed.

Or go and catch a falling star.

Bliss

Back in Missouri, I find the professor through a three-day foray on PerfectMatch.com. I write him. The correspondence that followed over less than four months from the last week in January to April 2007 fills 227 pages (I am not making this up either) of almost totally his words while I was in Missouri and he, in Baltimore. Yes, I did meet him. I did return to D.C. We did become lovers ever so briefly.

He loves the phrase "aesthetic bliss."

He refers to Nabokov's use of the word though he never identified the exact source: "an essay," he said. But I know that the phrase comes from Nabokov's afterword for *Lolita*:

> There are gentle souls who would pronounce Lolita meaningless because it does not teach them anything. I am neither a reader nor a writer of didactic fiction, and, despite John Ray's [Nabokov's fictional writer of the foreword to the novel] assertion, Lolita has no moral in tow. For me a work of fiction exists only in so far as it affords me what I shall bluntly call aesthetic bliss, that is a sense of being somehow, somewhere, connected with other states of being where art (curiosity, tenderness, kindness, ecstasy) is the norm.

In "On Involuntary Bliss," Nietzsche closes with this: *Zarathustra laughed to his heart, and said mockingly: "Happiness runs after me. That is because I do not run after women. For happiness is a woman."*

Nietzsche also loves the word bliss. He uses it twenty-six times in Thus Spoke Zarathustra.

On the first day and evening in early 2007 when I "virtually" met the professor, he wrote me ten e-mails that filled twenty-eight single-spaced pages. Yes, I saved them all.

Read this: "When you actually read my profile, you'll see that you are exactly what I'm looking for, because the core of what I'm looking for, beyond being able to share 'aesthetic bliss' with her is this: 'If you're the one, I want an evolving [i.e., lifelong, unending], deepening conversation with you in which we use all the verbal and physical resources we have, to know and be known—the good, the bad, and the fabulous. We could also use a shared joke, a simpatico sense of humor and irony about life, and us.' Yeah, I know, we haven't gotten to the in the flesh physical yet (though I was building a pretty good mental image of that too as we were talking! And I printed out the largest image of your picture I could get from Perfectmatch, which I'm keeping beside my computer now to remind me every day of how good-looking you truly are). But otherwise, I experienced everything I'm talking about here in the profile in our conversation tonight. (By the way, I don't even have a 'cut' option when I go to my Match profile. So I've printed it, so I can snail mail it to you. Please give me your Columbia address: it's safe! I'm a thousand miles away! And I do want you to read the profile, because you will see in black and white how perfect you are for me, as I know you felt you obviously were in our conversation tonight.)

As you might guess, he was not perfect for me.

Do we really believe in the phrase "perfect for me"?

He was a deluge.

What follows is an actual description of my condo in D.C. on the night soon after I rejected the professor, a night in May or June, when I roasted a chicken.

I refer to myself in the third person. Is that more or less solipsistic?

More.

I do this because I need some distance from my foolishness—and the fact that I was then smitten by someone else.

She had to find the key to the windows. She didn't know that windows on the seventh floor needed keys. She had only opened one when she moved in during winter. These gizmos prevent the windows from being opened with a protrusion of metal that the key fits into. Turn it one way and the window won't open; turn it the other and the window will. She kept getting on and off the ladder to stick the key into a window, open it, jump back on the ladder and continue fanning the smoke alarm.

She still doesn't know what makes the sprinkler system actually go off. But she also knows that yelling "help" in her hallway while her smoke alarm is screaming bloody murder does not raise a soul on a Thursday night! It was Thursday for god's sake. Wasn't anyone home?

When it was all over and the chicken was sitting majestically crispy on the counter and ready to eat and she had sprinkled the chopped thyme into the juices and done the only basting Thomas Keller requires—at the very end while the chicken is resting—she by the way needed to lie down—she knew that she could take care of herself. She had after all saved a twelve story building from burning or being evacuated and cooked a chicken that was hot damn good for a man she was smitten with. And boy was she smitten.

But not with the professor by the time I move back from Missouri and into my condo in D.C.

When I reject the professor, he first excoriates me. He asserts that he *gets* me. How dare I reject him.

Then he analyzes me. And perhaps he is right. Here is his analysis:

"After all you'd been through, you naturally needed a 'fever dream,' an escape into passion on all levels, from chocolate-covered strawberries on—[I sent him these on Valentine's Day]. But your psyche was always aware of the danger of drowning in the flood, and eventually you therefore 'woke up' from the dream, and realized, like Marianne in S&S [he refers to Marianne in Jane Austen's *Sense and Sensibility*] and Don Quixote, after their emblematic fevers, that you have to come to terms with reality."

Here is Thomas Keller's recipe at Epicurious (epicurious.com) under *Mon Poulet Rôti*:

Ingredients
One 2- to 3-pound farm-raised chicken
Kosher salt and freshly ground black pepper
2 teaspoons minced thyme (optional)
Unsalted butter
Dijon mustard

Preparation

Preheat the oven to 450°F. Rinse the chicken, then dry it very well with paper towels, inside and out. The less it steams, the drier the heat, the better.

Salt and pepper the cavity, then truss the bird. Trussing is not difficult, and if you roast chicken often, it's a good technique to feel comfortable with. When you truss a bird, the wings and legs stay close to the body; the ends of the drumsticks cover the top of the breast and keep it from drying out. Trussing helps the chicken to cook evenly, and it also makes for a more beautiful roasted bird.

Now, salt the chicken—I like to rain the salt over the bird so that it has a nice uniform coating that will result in a crisp, salty, flavorful skin (about 1 tablespoon). When it's cooked, you should still be able to make out the salt baked onto the crisp skin. Season to taste with pepper.

Place the chicken in a sauté pan or roasting pan and, when the oven is up to temperature, put the chicken in the oven. I leave it alone—I don't baste it, I don't add butter; you can if you wish, but I feel this creates steam, which I don't want. Roast it until it's done, 50 to 60 minutes. Remove it from the oven and add the thyme, if using, to the pan. Baste the chicken with the juices and thyme and let it rest for 15 minutes on a cutting board.

Remove the twine. Separate the middle wing joint and eat that immediately. Remove the legs and thighs. I like to take off the backbone and eat one of the oysters, the two succulent morsels of meat embedded here, and give the other to the person I'm cooking with. But I take the chicken butt for myself. I could never understand why my brothers always fought over that triangular tip—until one day I got the crispy, juicy fat myself. These are the cook's rewards. Cut the breast down the middle and serve it on the bone, with one wing joint still attached to each. The preparation is not meant to be super-elegant. Slather the meat with fresh butter. Serve with mustard on the side and, if you wish, a simple green salad. You'll start using a knife and fork, but finish with your fingers, because it's so good.

A roast chicken prepared in one hour, tender, remarkable. Safe from fire. No alarm: Aesthetic bliss.

Nietzsche says, *With rope-ladders I have learned to climb to many a window; with swift legs, I climbed high masts; and to sit on high masts of knowledge seemed to me no small bliss* [sometimes translated as *happiness*]: *to flicker like small flames on high masts—a small light only and yet great comfort for shipwrecked sailors and castaways.*

11

Bird on a Wire

Before I began this story, I'd slept for three years: When husband D. left me, the writing stopped. But once again I am writing.

Bird out of the cage, bird on a wire.

Nietzsche says, *He who would learn to fly one day must first learn to stand and walk and run and climb and dance; one cannot fly into flying.*

I sleep a literal sleep and dream a dream I am certain was real and then unreal inside the dream: I looked out a window. Sky and water merged and in the mix I saw iridescent blue-black birds, yellow-blue-black fish all on limbs of trees. Through the glass, safe inside a house with a large kitchen, my pots hung again. But how could fish and fowl, light and small as they were come to my tree? How could they, so rare in size and startled color, come so close to me?

The Bartender

Nietzsche says, as he weighs the world in the last dream of the morning, *Sex: only for the wilted, a sweet poison; for the lion-willed, however, the great invigoration of the heart and the reverently reserved wine of wines.*

As I learn to stand and walk and run and climb and dance—*one cannot fly into flying*, I search. And yes, there was a bartender.

The bartender doesn't drink. He knows good wine and orders me good wine that I usually pay for. I am better able to pay than he or so I think. He is short with big hands. He polishes his finger nails with clear polish, beautiful hands that are larger than they should be for his frame. His hands draw me. He is short and he walks with a limp that also draws me—this last he doesn't know.

When I dream asleep—I say this because I dream awake—I dream my father, more often since my husband left me, more often since I began Internet dating. Here's a weird glimpse: I see in front of me my father's fingers curling up behind the towel rack in my bathroom, his disembodied fingers. I am not frightened. I am comforted. His hand. Not my husband's hand. My father's hand that reaches out of the cosmos, out of the unconscious mind to me.

It was May and my separated-over-two-years-then husband sends me this e-mail, breaking my heart:

"Tony Soter is the philosopher-winemaker we talked with on the patio of that great little B&B in Napa (the one run by the guys who knew my uncle in their hometown of Denison, Iowa)."

I don't know why he is writing except to tell me about good wines and indeed he includes an article about Tony Soter's wines. But his e-mail is followed by an odd postscript:

"P.S. You don't have to comment about breakfast. I've thought it for you."

What did he mean?

And then I realize that he's referring in the postscript to the fact that he wouldn't make love in the morning: didn't want to miss that great breakfast at the B&B. You and I (and he) know that a big refrigerator, not the one holding the eggs, milk, syrup, not the cornucopia Napa refrigerator but the metaphorical one (Oh, sure, call it the elephant if you like) sits inside the P.S. What I mean: When your girlfriend yells at you when you come home on the anniversary of the day you met, the day she expects you'll have flowers or will take her out for dinner, and she says, "You left the top off the milk again!" There's a refrigerator in the room that has nothing to do with milk.

Sex and D. are *my* problem.

The bartender helps me see the scope and size of that problem—in today's psychobabble vernacular—that *I own*.

The bartender took the free class I taught when I returned from Missouri after my stint as a visiting writer—my time out-of-town. I taught that class in the fall at the Martin Luther King Library that sits across the street from my condo. When the class was over, we met by chance at the Dana Gioia reading there. I'd told the class about it. The bartender wanted to chat when he arrived, the way he'd often seemed to want to chat when I'd seen him where he used to tend bar—a tony restaurant full of people from the Hill though it is not on the proverbial Hill.

Dana Gioia read and I bought *Interrogations at Noon*. I was struck throughout the reading how many times he mentioned his wife who was not present. She is a presence. I don't recall if he read these lines that evening, but the poem "Voyeur" lies next to the title poem in the book. I read it now:

> . . . and watching her undress across the room.
> oblivious of him, watching as her slip
> falls soundlessly and disappears in the shadow.

The opening ellipsis is his. The ellipsis that follows, as I take you to the last stanza, is mine:

But what he watches here is his own life.
He is the missing man, the loyal husband.
sitting in the room he craves to enter . . .

After the reading, I suggested to the bartender that we go over to Zaytinya for a drink and he managed to get me a free glass of wine (bartenders do this sort of thing for each other). A little alcohol and I told him about my heart.

My husband didn't watch me undress. He had not wanted to make love to me for the last decade of our marriage. He had kissed two women over two years in front of me. I don't mean a quick kiss. I mean the proverbial "making out." I did not, as I now know he wished I had, hit him over the head with the also proverbial frying pan. Yes, I am stuck in the kitchen of metaphors for absence of sex. But I did finally have to ask what was going on. And he did finally have to tell me that he wanted to live by himself. I had little other information. And I don't feel betrayed by the disloyalty for after all it was more about humiliation than about sex for me, the watcher, the voyeur.

When I read Dana Gioia, I wanted to give the understanding in that last stanza to my husband. Perhaps he craved to enter. I think I *know* he did, but I shall never know why he could not.

I don't recall how much of this I told the bartender, but I do recall that it was more than I should have. And in telling whatever I told my heart ached with the betrayal I committed and that I commit here with shameful impunity. I live in the shame of the betrayal that sets me free: I *write* it.

The bartender is kind.

There's an edge of anger underneath that I now know comes out of a privileged and brutal childhood. His father beat him. He was the oldest and he got beaten the most. He doesn't drink for good reason. I don't know exactly the reason, but I know he's seen a troubled world, saved a woman and her child only to end up in jail falsely accused of abusing her. He got out but not because his wealthy mother bailed him. He was in jail longer than was fair: innocent and jailed. What can make up for that?

The bartender limps because he has had one hip replaced. The other hip must wait for his strength to build. He is strong: a beautiful upper body even if the whole body is not in proportion. I am attracted to the flawed body—not the yellowed teeth (cigars and who knows what), those teeth, too big for the handsome face. He is a mixed bag.

My father was an ugly man. His nose and his ears were way too big for his face and his thinness when young made both flaws more prominent. Plastic surgery after he married my beautiful mother and had me and my sister, made him not handsome but close.

The bartender writes me:

"I sat on the train tonight amongst the post New Year's Eve revelers. The air was redolent with alcohol and the intermittent sounds of slurred conversations. I caught a couple of glances and realize I appeared a sad case stoically reading my book alone while multiple groups and couples were continuing their festivities and going to places where, no doubt, with the lubrication of alcohol and the enhancement of narcotics, astronomically bad decisions would be made. I did not look like a guy who had spent an evening full of joy, stimulation, great food and sex—albeit in a censored form but no less erotic for that—and tenderness with a beautiful woman who really wanted me in her bed. How appearances can deceive. A quick inventory of the car: More than a few of my fellow travelers' evenings would end badly—breakups and brawls, lost keys and wallets, 'You have the right to remain silent,' strange beds and ER rooms in the offing; but yours truly was going home to savor the memory of your body, the taste of your lips, the down of your sex in my hand, and the look in your eyes that told me you were, once again, better than okay. My evening was priceless and perfect; and I knew in my heart I would feel great about it in the morning."

Yes, he touched me, the bartender who will write his own book. Oh, let me live to see that.

I reject him, ultimately, because (do I know for sure?) because I fear the anger inside him, because he doesn't handle dating with panache and shamefully that is important to me, or more likely, the closer he got, the more I wanted my husband and my father. He is neither.

Broken Glass

When we got married, D. crushed the glass. Any glass may be used for the Jewish wedding glass—even a light bulb. Couples often choose a special glass to be broken and kept. Like the light bulb, that glass is wrapped in a cloth napkin (to avoid shattered glass shards). At the end of the ceremony, the groom stomps on the glass to great applause.

I am writing about the wreckage of a marriage. Restate: The wreckage of *my* marriage. *My marriage.* The paradox is clear: no marriage is owned by one of the partners.

How do I judge who was at fault?

I think of Japanese jurors. I've saved a *New York Times* article from July 16, 2007 that appeared on the front page. Japan was attempting to move to jury trials, but the jurors in a mock trial were reluctant to express their opinions.

> They never engaged one another in discussion. Their opinions had to be extracted by the judges and were often hedged by the Japanese language's rich ambiguity... Under the proposed system, randomly chosen citizens will sit on the bench next to judges, decide cases together and hand out sentences.

Reasons given for the reluctance of jurors: respect for authority, submissiveness as part and parcel of the national character.

I thought fiction would give me my due. So I began to write a story about the bartender. Here is the fragment of the story:

The bartender said to the woman he was with, a buxom blonde, taller than he, while he fiddled with a book, a novel, Fitzgerald she guessed from the Fitz that showed on the spine, though mostly she noticed how large his hand was on the binding of the book, "Nothing is sexier than a woman in a man's button-down, in my button-down. You oughta know that by now." So, they were lovers.

She watched from her table in the Martin Luther King library where she sat with her legal brief, the one she didn't know how to write, that damn environmental stuff that she was always on the wrong side of at Dewey LeBeouf, her law firm around the corner from the library. She'd leave in the evening to escape the corporate banter, to try to figure out how the hell to defend Big Oil. When he looked her way, when his glance hung there for a bit, she smiled and was sure she'd never see him again.

But there he was behind the bar at Kincaids when she ordered the Kendall Jackson red Zinfandel and he said, "A ways from the library tonight, huh?"

"The library?" She wasn't about to admit she had noticed him. She was in enough trouble. Her lover of ten years had moved out of their condo last week and informed her they would need to sell it. She was about to be homeless. Oh, she knew that she could find a place, but she felt like a baby left out on a doorstep. She felt childish, worse than childish: infantile. Abandoned. She wanted to say it out loud to the bartender. I'm abandoned.

"Would you like to look at a menu?" The bartender resumed his professional stance, turned to get her the expensive glass of wine and she saw that he walked with a distinct limp, a kind of wobble as if one side of his body were more heavily weighted than the other. She noticed that he was short. He had seemed so tall at the library when he spoke so firmly to the blonde with what she viewed as one of the most seductive lines she'd ever heard. Okay, maybe not. Maybe the truth was it was a sentence she wished Guy had said to her. Who goes out, anyway, with a guy named Guy? she asked herself as she sipped the red wine he had now handed her and stood before her with a menu in his hand. Those hands again. She was in love with his hands.

"Parapraxes," she said, "is what I need and I'll take the menu."

"So, you need to forget?"

"How would you know what I need?"

"Parapraxes. You said that. But what you really need are the fried clams."

You should know here what she is not saying even to herself: Guy has not made love to her for five of their ten years together without great effort on her part that includes his rejection of her La Perla garter belt and bra that set her back a pretty penny and that ended making her feel less than pretty, and yes, believe it or not, she is quite a dish and knows it.

Why did she stay? That is the question.

She would tell you that last night she dreamed she was in the courtroom without a script, that she opened her mouth and nothing came out in front of the judge, in front of the jury, in front of her colleagues, that she searched her mind for the quote she'd use and all she could come up with was Charlie Parker's line, *If you haven't lived it, it won't come out of your horn.*

I wrote that and went outside. A black SUV with blackened windows moved off. Its rear window shattered onto the asphalt with no apparent cause except the startle of the engine. Tiny pieces of broken glass, each one a perfect triangle lay where I stood. The SUV stopped mid-street. No one got out. It moved ahead.

This is my subject: The broken glass, the wake.

As for parapraxes: Get this. D. lost his wedding ring in September, a month before the galleys of my book came out, a month before he kissed my friend after a party—It was not merely a kiss; they were making out on the couch while I washed dishes in the kitchen. I stood behind the couch and watched. Then I went outside and waited.

If you want to know the truth about the bartender, read backwards: I wrote about him. If you want to know *the truth*, look elsewhere or get you to a Japanese jury.

Adultery

When my daughter turned thirty-five—a beautiful startling woman whose mind is full of wonder—she suggested I look for a man I might have known when I was single: either before I married her father or between my marriages, before I married D. "You never know," she said, "who might still be single or divorced or widowed."

On the day of my daughter's birth, I counted the months. She was born in February, my sister's birth month. January, when my mother died in 1990. March, when I turned 63. June, when my sister died in 1993. She was 53.

I am discovering what it is not only to age but to live a decade longer than my older sibling. My sister would have helped through heartbreak. She knew it well. That knowing I have now learned is a gift.

My daughter is a philosopher. For this reason and others, I find her advice worth sleeping on.

I dreamt I'd taken my first philosophy class with Jacques Derrida. My daughter is an expert in this philosopher who died in 2004. I was taking the final exam and could not answer a single question. The test was full of quotes from philosophers I should have read but had not and from some I had read but still did not recognize what they had said. The key was to match the quotes with the names, no list of names provided. Others taking the exam seemed to be finishing but I left every question blank with the exception of one guess: Nietzsche, who said, *It is not a lack of love, but a lack of friendship that makes unhappy marriages.*

I am learning the meaning of that sentence and perhaps more important the meaning of heartbreak.

Perhaps I should call j., a man I'd "dated," the man from the number five bus—I *thought* he was single—after my first husband and I divorced. I dated D. during this time as well—he *was* single.

I did call j.

Then I slept and dreamt: His eyes in the dream were cloud-white blue, the color of D.'s eyes. When I woke I knew that my memory of who he was or might have been was a vision of him but not him.

j's eyes are brown. Those eyes once electrified me. But he had never been totally real. He was not possible. I'd met him before I married D. and fallen madly for him only to discover later to my horror that j. was married. The serial adulterer I'd often write about in my stories, the man I'd always believed had broken my heart before I knew what breaks a heart. That I learned from D., the man I would always love even if I could never be with him again, even if I could never sleep with him again—all the things I was certain of and this from a woman who is certain of only one thing: the meaning of an open heart. And this term "open heart" is one I can't define. So even that certainty is surrounded by uncertainty.

Definitions are not my strong suit.

In the dream j., an attorney, was on trial and I had inexplicably been chosen to be his attorney. But I had not been to law school. I was patently unqualified but there was no way out. He had been accused of stealing cigarettes kept in cartons in the office of his closet, kept under lock and key so that no one in the office could smoke them. J. used to be a chain smoker and a self-claimed alcoholic (I never believed that he drank enough to be one, but he had a coin in his pocket, a five-year coin he'd shown me that alcoholics carry after being sober for that long). We were in the courtroom. I was trying to figure out how to solve the case. I decided, perhaps because of too much television, that lawyers must be detectives, at least criminal lawyers did. I was only interested in crimes of passion and anger. Crimes of need fell into categories that covered the global realm of the human psyche while crimes of passion and anger were primal. Or so I thought. I was not certain of this or anything but the open heart.

I concluded he was innocent of the crime of stealing the cigarettes because that crime was not one of need—not for him anyway. It had to be a crime of anger or passion against him. I knew he was having an affair with an Asian beauty, a young attorney in his office.

I had learned this while awake—a phone call, a drink with j., the man I thought I'd once loved. And of course he was still married but told me he'd left his wife. Left his wife for someone other than me? How could he?

But, as in the dream, I would defend him.

Open heart, open heart, open heart.

His wife is a beauty in her own right, a beauty whom he said he *loved* but didn't *like*.

But what did he know of love? This I am concluding about myself so I say it about him. Most people come to such conclusions through their own clouded lenses that lack the clarity of cloud-white blue.

j. had not joined the Asian attorney though he was still sleeping with her: "The sex is amazing." That's what he said when we met for the drink. That was the sort of thing he said out loud while I drank red wine and he drank water, the sort of thing he should say only to the woman he was having sex with, the sort of thing that made me see that he'd not been the one to break my heart, that there is a difference between disappointment and rejection and that irreparable break in the beating organ at the center of our chests and minds and souls—the metaphor for who we are: human and alive: open heart, open heart, open heart.

And I saw that Nietzsche is right about marriage.

Frying Pans

Charade: The Oxford English Dictionary (I own it: all seventeen volumes that include the supplements for my edition) notes that Thackeray (William Makepeace: don't you love his middle name? A command to be taken to heart) used the word in *Vanity Fair* in 1848: *The performers disappeared to get ready for the second charade-tableau.*

After Becky Sharp has achieved the coup of marriage in chapter XVI, our narrator notes that *the children dressed themselves and acted plays.*

And so I dress myself and act in my play in search of a happy ending: I'm a sucker for wishing that does some good.

Becky Sharp's story of social climbing struck me as particularly grim and nothing like the fairy tale she sought—or the one that I am after. One concludes she would have kissed anyone to get where she could be.

Are you wondering if the princess does not kiss the "Frog-Prince," what then does she do? There are two versions, plus the one Disney has provided, the kiss fulfilled, but whose roots lie with those grim brothers.

In *The Complete Grimm's Fairy Tales* that I own based on the translation by Margaret Hunt, the princess, ordered by her ethical father to honor her word, must take the frog to bed with her. Instead, she places him in the corner of her bedroom. The frog says, *"I am tired, I want to sleep as well as you, lift me up or*

I will tell your father." At this she was terribly angry, and took him up and threw him with all her might against the wall. "*Now you be quiet, odious frog.*"

And with this angry and aggressive act upon his being, the frog becomes the prince. But this is not the end of the story.

There is no end to the ways a woman may hit a man over the head with a frying pan.

Oh, how good I am at this. I *write* it.

I have been reading and re-reading Joyce's *Ulysses* when a married man, w., who knows I am separated calls me.

I look at the rug in my condo through the bottom of my wine glass, watch the last of the wine slosh to the edge of the glass and through the glass see the blur of another rug that was the first thing D. and I had bought and that he now owns. I see *home* distorted through the bottom of the glass.

The man who calls is a reader of Joyce. He tells me he would like to name my private part "Molly." Here is the fantasy: Perhaps he will fall in love, leave his wife?

He says to me who has lost and who has waited and who wants sex, who wants to be cocked, cooked, corked by him who might be kind or not—I think I don't care. I'd waited long and looked through the glass, through the wine darkly.

I meet him briefly during the day. He cannot meet me in the evening. He picks me up in his Jaguar, drives me to the Potomac River front.

When we walk along the river that afternoon he picks a penny from the grass and gives it to me after I show it to him lying there in the grass. I, speak of "seeing," because I want to be *seen*. He places the penny in my palm and now it is in my pocket, warm from his hand that he wanted between my legs, the man I resisted—but it is getting harder to do.

And penance and grief (Ulysses, 11.1030), misquoting Joyce and thinking of the penance I should do but I am unrepentant. I think, Free. His hand between my legs, a man who wants me, a man whose cock gets cocked for me. That's the sin I want. I'm in grief but not penitent. A new experience.

And I have underwear.

After the D.-kissing-of-the-second-girlfriend—let us call it the second incident—I went to Neiman Marcus and spent 1500 bucks on La Perla underwear. And it wasn't as hard as you might think to spend that much money on underwear and not as much underwear as you might think.

On underwear, I offer this probably apocryphal story about Florenz Ziegfeld and his Follies: When asked why he bought expensive silk underwear for all his chorus girls, underwear that never was seen by the audience, Flo answered, "The girls know."

I told D. what I'd bought and how much I'd spent.

There are many ways to hit a man over the head with a frying pan.

Ah, I am more aggressive than I pretend to be or like to think I am: In my shopping and most certainly in my fantasies.

I believe the girls may *know*, but that men care little for underwear because that's what I'd learned. I now hope for men who would be boys. I think the dirty thought when I read *Big Benaben. Big Benben.* (Ulysses, 11.53) Time tolls for Bloom and me. Cocked not corked but easily cocked for me, I dream, while Bloom wanders and Molly and Blazes go at it.

The *false priest.* (Ulysses, 11.1016) What did that mean? Did she need a priest, a shrink? *Virgin should say: or fingered only* (Ulysses, 11.1086). I want to be fingered, not in despair but in the joy of being: A flute alive and I once played the flute but didn't want to be played the way I'd been played—with practiced touch. No. I want a man who would see me as a flute that has been waiting to be played.

The other version of the "Frog-Prince can be found at Authorama:

> [T]he king said to the young princess, 'As you have given your word you must keep it; so go and let him in.' She did so, and the frog hopped into the room, and then straight on—tap, tap—plash, plash—from the bottom of the room to the top, till he came up close to the table where the princess sat. 'Pray lift me upon the chair,' said he to the princess, 'and let me sit next to you.' As soon as she had done this, the frog said, 'Put your plate nearer to me, that I may eat out of it.' This she did, and when he had eaten as much as he could, he said, 'Now I am tired; carry me upstairs, and put me into your bed.' And the princess, though very unwilling, took him up in her hand, and put him upon the pillow of her own bed, where he slept all night long. As soon as it was light he jumped up, hopped downstairs, and went out of the house. 'Now, then,' thought the princess, 'at last he is gone, and I shall be troubled with him no more.'
> But she was mistaken; for when night came again she heard the same tapping at the door; and the frog came once more, and said:
>   'Open the door, my princess dear,

Open the door to thy true love here!
And mind the words that thou and I said
By the fountain cool, in the greenwood shade.'
And when the princess opened the door the frog came in, and slept upon her pillow as before, till the morning broke. And the third night he did the same. But when the princess awoke on the following morning she was astonished to see, instead of the frog, a handsome prince, gazing on her with the most beautiful eyes she had ever seen, and standing at the head of her bed.

Three times in her bed, the magic number that broke the spell.

I am drawn to the toss-on-the-wall story perhaps because *when wishing still did some good,* I'd wished for the proverbial frying pan. More because the story ends with another anecdote about the king's servant Faithful Henry, so distraught at the king's dilemma that he caused three iron bands to be laid around his heart.

I wish for Faithful Henry.

In the charade that continues here and that was my life, here is what happened:

And then I dated. And then I worried that I would become Becky Sharp, that I would find and give in to money and status over love, that I would not recognize the frog-prince.

Hypersensitive

Stock market crashed. No noise. Economy in dire straits.

Robert Rauschenberg died on May 12, 2008 at the age of eighty-two. That day I walked over to see his work at the Portrait Gallery near my apartment.

I saved the obit., got caught in the web of memory. My own straits.

My father's white shirt, the ribbed, sleeveless undershirt beneath that as a small child I carried with me: "her schmata," my mother called it. My father's photo taken by my daughter when she was studying photography in high school, developing her own pictures in Bethesda Chevy Chase High School's darkroom, hangs on the first wall to my left as I enter my bedroom in the loft where I live and write in downtown D.C. He is holding his pipe, one finger tamping down the tobacco, the can of Amphora nearby. The photo is black and white and my memory of him, faded to tone. He, a decade gone this June 6, eighty-four and crippled from Parkinson's disease and a broken hip when he died. He comes to me like his home movies, overexposed, so much light that I can barely see him. Rauschenberg-white: my father's white dress shirt. "I always thought of the white paintings as being not passive but very—well, hypersensitive," Rauschenberg said. The schmata shirt beneath the dress shirt.

My 82-year-old father called me in the middle of the night before he died and in the anguish of aging, asked: "What am I here for?"—a despairing cry that expressed the humility of existence and underscored the imperative of continuing to ask the question even as the darkness moves across us. It is the autobiographical tautological question that starts and ends where it begins.

My father took my hand, and said, "There's an inevitability about the present."

I understood the way I'd understood when my mother, four years after her stroke, decided not to eat when the new year came, when she took my hand and said "Yitgadal v'yitkadash"—the first two words of the mourner's Kaddish. It was five years later when my father took my hand one hot day in June.

We'd been sitting in the house with the old round Toastmaster fan blowing at our feet, humming the way old memories did inside my head. We'd been talking about the kind of housing called "assisted living." "Assisted living," he said. "Funny term. Either you're living or you're not, right?"

I didn't answer.

"I'm on my way down," my father said. "I know that. This is just a stopover."

"Stopover from what to what?"

"Don't get philosophical on me, kid."

My father's eyes were brown like mine. I saw them full of light from the sun that angled through the window. I saw the green and yellow—the colors of my mother's hazel eyes—there inside the brown. I remembered my dream after my mother died. In a haze of yellow light, my mother in a flowered housedress. I couldn't tell the color of her hair—pure white when she died. But it must be dark—around her face in finger-placed waves, how it was when I could still fit beneath her arm, lean against her curve of breast. Then an empty chair. An elegant, suited man on the sidewalk. My mother, on the stoop of their row house. Her arm raised high in dance position. No one stands inside her hold. She leans to unheard sound. She turns round. A fox-trot circle. My father threads eight-millimeter film through the projector, on the wheel. A home movie. Overexposed. My mother. Like the whiteness of a leafing tree against night sky.

"Why are you crying?" my father said. "This won't be the last time you see me."

"It's what I do. I cry, easily, often."

"So do I," he said. "It's inherited."

Hypersensitive.

I have looked for him in every man I've dated during the last three years—the years of separation. I sensed him one Saturday night in the expert on eastern European economics with big ears like my father's, knew he might kiss me when he offered his tamarind soda a second time as we ate a late dinner, if you call what we settled on *dinner*, at Oyamel after seeing a new Claude Lalouch film, yes, that Claude of *A Man and a Woman*, a movie this sixty-six year-old, tall lanky man had seen at the Circle Theater, a D.C. relic, razed now. I saw it with my father when it first hit theaters, had Netflixed it two weeks before meeting this man.

Was the camera hand-held? as Lelouch circles round the lovers as they meet on the train platform after they'd parted, after she'd said she could not make love because of the memory of her dead husband. Her lover, rebuffed, left her. She took the train. He rethought on the drive back in the Mustang, met her train. Francis Lai's soundtrack strikes me now as sentimental, but, like a memory, Lai's rhythm and the humming singers resound, will not be resisted. No rational thought. No editing. No chance to cut the sweet and to the core where I like to be.

When I danced with my husband, I once upon a time hummed. D. has perfect pitch, a curse and a blessing. For me, a curse. For him too I now think: To have heard those off-notes from my throat, the vibration of my vocal chords gone wrong, not tuned. Off pitch. No humming allowed. Not on that chest where I lay my head when we danced. This man says he is working on the question, "Who am I?" while I wait.

T. S. Eliot tells us,

> We shall not cease from exploration
> And the end of all our exploring
> Will be to arrive where we started
> And know the place for the first time.

That Saturday night at Oyamel, the economics expert offers me the tamarind soda on first pour (I refuse) and then offers again after he's drunk half. My father and I shared chocolate soda and coddies at the drugstore soda fountain on Dolfield Avenue, three blocks from Grantley Road where I grew up in Baltimore. We'd walk there together, wait for my mother who was getting her hair done at the salon next door.

Lanky man's tamarind soda doesn't measure up to his memory when he was in the Peace Corp in Columbia where the beans were refried more times than his strong stomach could bear and where he went into town for a tin of cookies and the soda, ate the whole tin, sloshed back the soda. I taste the second-hand and secondary soda, the hint of spice and tart rind that recalls my mother's glazed orange peel that my father and I would have at home after the coddies and mustard on saltines.

This man had held my hand on the first date, not again on this Saturday night, not once in the movie or while we walked. That first date, one glass of wine and nothing much to eat at the Tabard Inn (nothing much to eat this night either. Is he cheap? my daughter asked.) Did I care?

Later I did care. My daughter began referring to him as "Cheapskate" after I took him to dinner at Tosca and it seemed only fair that I should pay. I ordered a bottle of wine. He did not object. He ordered the salad, an appetizer, the pasta, the dessert. The thin man *did* eat when he was not paying the check.

Thank goodness I was not dating him as the economic crisis deepened. Would he dare even to go out?

But his quiet, his calm like the sense of the sea receding with the tide; his angles like my father's, a Giacometti sculpture in shadow at the edge of sand in fading light.

That first date we descended the escalator at Dupont Circle, knowing that we would go down together to separate at the platform. He'd said, "Ah, so I get to hold your hand for a bit more?" as we descended the long arc down. The slight lift in his voice as if it were a question though we were palm on palm all the way down as he recalled a scene from the movie *Risky Business*: the departing train through the narrowing perspective of track on track, a camera's eye in his words, the sound of sex in his voice: Rebecca Mornay and Tom Cruise making love on the train, politely unspoken between us.

He had not touched me since that first palm-on-palm moment. The afternoon he'd called with his "research," as he called it from the website Rotten Tomatoes, reviews of movies playing at the E Street Theater, the first on his list, *Roman De Gare*, "Claude Lalouch," he said. "That Claude," I said and named that movie we'd both seen in 1967. "Ah, yes," he said. I didn't know Lalouch was still around. I cast my net back to the year I turned twenty-one. "Let alone alive," I said. And so we chose the third-date movie.

After Oyamel, two tapas (hearts of palm salad and two scallops, the soda and a licorice tea), he walks me to my loft where I fob the glass front doors open. "Would you like to walk me up?" "I could do that." We ride in the elevator, apart, then a short walk to my door. I turn the key. The bolt slides open with the click of certainty. I turn my back to the door. He is 6'2''. I am 5'5''. He bends, a curve of slender grace as he slides his hand behind my head and he kisses me. I kiss him and then again. He holds me against his chest, his arm around my back. "You are a sweet man," I say into the knit of his cashmere sweater, my childhood cheek against my father's heart, the white shirt, the soft-ribbed undershirt beneath.

17

Cinderella

Nietzsche says, *Deep yellow and hot red: thus **my** taste wants it; it mixes blood into all colors. But whosoever whitewashes his house betrays a whitewashed soul to me.*

Blood runs red in "Cinderella": *"No one shall be my wife but she whose foot this golden slipper fits."* When the shoe will not fit the eldest stepsister, *her mother gave her a knife and said, "Cut the toe off; when you are Queen you will have no more need to go on foot."*

And the blood trickles from her foot and her sister's, also cut to fit the slipper.

Cinderella has lost her father to her evil stepmother: Her father does not protect her.

I find the psychiatrist on Match.com. I find a man who I do not realize strikingly resembles my father. My daughter points this out to me on meeting him, one month after he and I have met.

In the e-mail exchanges to arrange our blind date—Internet dates *are* blind, despite the posted photo—he offers to cook dinner for me. I refuse and he is gracious. We meet at Bistro D'Oc: the restaurant is close to me and feels safe. I see him on 10th Street waiting: The angle of his nose, the length of his face—a large gentle face—his height, more than six feet, his thinness. We kiss on meeting. A quick but decisive kiss on the mouth. He orders a bottle of 2006 Croze-Hermitage Syrah at dinner. He comes around the table at the end of dinner and kisses me.

I swoon.

I send him the sonnet in Act I of *Romeo and Juliet* before their first kiss (rhyming as all Shakespeare's sonnets do in this manner: abab, cdcd, efef, gg):

> **Rom. [To Juliet]** If I profane with my unworthiest hand
> This holy shrine, the gentle sin is this,
> My lips, two blushing pilgrims, ready stand
> To smooth that rough touch with a tender kiss.
> **Jul.** Good pilgrim, you do wrong your hand too much
> Which mannerly devotion shows in this.
> For saints have hands that pilgrims' hands do touch,
> And palm to palm is holy palmers' kiss.
> **Rom.** Have not saints lips, and holy palmers too?
> **Jul.** Ay, pilgrim, lips that they must use in prayer.
> **Rom.** Oh then, dear saint, let lips do what hands do.
> They pray. Grant thou, lest faith turn to despair.
> **Jul.** Saints do not move, though grant for prayers' sake.
> **Rom.** Then move not while my prayer's effect I take.
> Thus, from my lips by thine my sin is purged. [Kissing her]

My father celebrated his birthday in my youth on August 12 before he learned when I was grown—a search for his birth certificate—that he was born on July 28. D. is born August 2. The psychiatrist's birthday is within one day of August 12.

I swoon.

He does not whitewash his house, his soul: He tells me that while in training, he took a medical student's Rorschach test that revealed he was psychotic. He tells me he has been accused of violence, unfairly jailed, a restraining order. He has been married four times, is in the process of divorcing his fourth wife. He is a psychiatrist who has never been analyzed because he did not need to be analyzed.

I send W.H. Auden:

> *At last the secret is out, as it always must come in the*
> *end,*
> *The delicious story is ripe to tell to the intimate friend;*
> . . .

There is always another story, there is more than
meets the eye.

. . .

There is always a wicked secret, a private reason for
this.

I have lived with Oh-So-Greta-Garbo: "I need to be alone," he said, and then he left with all his secrets.

The psychiatrist writes me: "You take my breath away, and return it refreshed. You breathe from my mouth, from my chest so as to restore life that could have died from a too-early birth."

I send Wallace Stevens:

His self and the sun were one
And his poems, although makings of his self
Were no less makings of the sun.

He goes to his house in Florida to plant roses. I read Rilke who is said to have died from the prick of a rose thorn and the leukemia that it revealed when the wound would not heal:

The Bowl of Roses
. . . But now you know how to forget such things,
for now before you stands the bowl of roses,
unforgettable and wholly filled
with attainable being and promise,
a gift beyond anyone's giving, a presence
that might be ours and our perfection.

He writes me from Florida:

"He sits in the restaurant across from the Aztec princess, pretending he's in a Chinese buffet in Sarasota, pretending he doesn't have tears in his eyes sine die, pretending he doesn't see his fate and that he doesn't know his future.

"He pretends that he doesn't say to her that he realizes he has no cure for any of the many of them, and not even that he wasn't put on Earth to be a healer-priest. He does realize that he doesn't have to cure any of it, that it shall be more than sufficient to be with all of them as with himself at the scene and at the time, to touch, to be inside her. He knows she knows. He falls into the Charlie Chan pit as they press the button that upends his bench but he's still there, and the Aztec princess now has the bronze knife in her hand.

"He has a moment of dread, then pretends he doesn't, and then he doesn't. He doesn't have to pretend: he knows that it isn't trust if it's safe. So he kisses her, and he doesn't have to pretend about that, nor that she doesn't kiss him back.

"Then she picks up the knife again, gently cuts the buttons from his shirt. Eyes touch. She plunges the knife into his chest. Blood all over, and she holds his pulsing slippery heart in her hands, raises it to her mouth to make him immortal, bites deeply. His blood drips from her chin, the owner approves of her appetite: a fine cassoulet he is.

"He doesn't have to pretend that it doesn't hurt, that he has no fear.

"Je comprend. Et alors, je t'aime en plus."

I am frightened. But he explains. He has read my story "Sine Die" that appears in my book *The Woman Who Never Cooked.* He responds to the story. I have misunderstood.

I have had one dinner date with him at Bistro D'Oc and known him five days. I eat strings beans Szechuan at Eat First on H Street. On the Chinese calendar I am the dog, he is the snake. "Beware the snake," the Chinese placemat tells me from the table.

He has *read* me.

The man I loved read all my work. When the galley proofs arrived for the book, the man I loved kissed my friend while I washed dishes in the kitchen.

I believe that paradox is the struggle of existence, that love absolves paradox, however briefly. I believe in the numinous quality of existence.

How do we know what we are seeing?

What you are perceiving about me seems bifurcated. You think you *know* the story. What you are seeing is the paradox of my needs and yours.

No one can provide anyone else perfect safety. But two people may provide moments of perfection that build on one another and that give them a sense of connection in the world, the sense, the belief that "again" will occur, with all the risks of existence, with all the changeable nature of the all too human.

We are blind when we believe we *know* the other's story.

Cinderella wishes: A bird, not a fairy godmother, comes to Cinderella's tree that grew from the water of her tears on the grave of her mother.

Her stepsisters are *punished with blindness all their days.*

How to see the other's story? That is the question. And the answer is, as Nietzsche says, *Whoever would become light and a bird . . .*

Something Old for Something New

When the groom stomps on the glass, some say, he recalls the destruction of the temple or announces the creation of two bodies, one mind.

Something blue, something borrowed, something old for something new.

The loss of a marriage is the loss of habeas corpus: When the two parties decide to separate, one of them pleads with the other for a writ of habeas corpus. One of them must believe, or both perhaps, that he is imprisoned and unfairly so. He asks his warden to justify his incarceration. I am no longer sure who was asking whom in my marriage. But I am sure that what had been created was annihilated.

And then I met the psychiatrist. After two weeks, the psychiatrist wants my passwords to my computer and e-mail. The psychiatrist wants my schedule. He prepares a paper with every day of the week and the hours during the day. He asks me to fill it in. I do not.

He uses pale orange nylon fishing string to hang his glasses on his neck. I admire this clever elegant solution to a difficult problem. He burns the knot on the end of string for each stem of my reading glasses.

I think: fisherman's blood knot.

He measures my wrist and ring finger while I sleep. He burns a knot for the string he places on my wrist. I refuse to wear the string ring. He burns the knot for the string on his wrist and for the string he places on his left hand, ring finger.

He tells me we will marry on March 21 next year.

I sleep and dream: In the dream, the man I am married to has canceled my Amex Card and was able to because I didn't know he had control of the account. I didn't know it was *his* account. How could that be? I pay the bills. Mine is the only name on the account. So I called and was told I had to meet a person in-person to fix this. I got in a cab and asked, "Do you know where an AmEx office is?" And the cab driver took me. A homely woman, pale in skin, dark in hair but with the pallor of someone who rarely goes outside, the pallor of someone who works on the phone all the time, who does things that hurt others, the pallor of a person who knows that she does such work and who hates it but does it anyway, the pallor of resignation, says, "Yes, the card is canceled. Your husband canceled it." I said, "Reinstate my card." She said, instead of "no," "Your husband doesn't like questions, he doesn't like to be questioned."

The psychiatrist does not treat patients. He decides who shall stay in hospital and who shall not: Insurance work. Other doctors call him to ask who shall be covered and who shall not, who shall stay and who shall go.

We met in March.

By the end of April: Emergency egress: (not in order; order, not possible): I had to have a locksmith, H&H Locksmith to change the lock on my condo. Heaven and Hell? He became so angry in Boston where we'd gone to meet my daughter and son-in-law that I called a cab to get myself to the airport. When I tell him this, he gets in the rented convertible, whose top he never took down, guns it out and into the circular driveway four times, maybe five, once with my luggage that he put in the trunk. I get him *once* to stop and pop the trunk. Now I *have* my luggage. The taxi I had called with a North End Italian hairdresser-as-part-time cabby arrives: she throws my luggage into her trunk, tells me to get in, power locks the doors. We wait and watch him gun the engine and drive towards us. She has her finger on her cell—"We may need the cops," she says. But he drives away, gunning that gas pedal harder than all the other times. The cabby drives me to Logan airport, asks, "You got a ticket?" The shrink has my ticket.

It costs 500 bucks to fly on the same day from Logan to Reagan.

He was angry because I would not tell him what my daughter had said after the four of us had had lunch in The Charles Hotel: wonderful buffet. Concern about the string. Her sense that I am in danger.

He records our last phone call, transcribes it and e-mails it to me. I cannot know if it is totally accurate. Here is the e-mail:

> I cannot be with you. My conclusion is that we cannot be together.
>
> [I am not convinced that I subscribe to that.]
>
> Don't chase me. You deserve more dignity than that.
>
> [You have a deep friend here and if you recalculate your conclusion I want you to let me know that]
>
> Your generosity and your woundedness—
>
> [my hurts that I carry with me. It was my inability to find out what you thought or what you were feeling after your phone call with Sarah that drove me frantic.]
>
> Sarah is not what needs more healing.
>
> [You have been generous enough to tell me that you're all mixed up. So am I in my own way].
>
> You deserve someone better. Someone better will come along for you. You are a deeply caring man.
>
> [God damn you. You finally made me reject you, or fail you.]
>
> I don't feel rejected. I'm not made to be able to deal with how you were, acted yesterday.
>
> [It doesn't matter how I ended it. I finally failed one of your tests.]
>
> Logistics (We discuss the transfer of items in my apartment and his. We each are to leave them in the lobby of my condo. I have thrown away his toothbrush and a penile ring).
>
> [I'm shocked that you would throw away anything of mine]
>
> I'm so sorry for that.
>
> [I will end this conversation by saying that you are the dearest person to me.]

We were not done.

He takes a class I taught at The Smithsonian for four Saturdays in the month of May. He would be on the bench outside when I arrived thirty minutes early to be "miked," to set up slides. He did not speak. He did not do the assignments. He did not open his book.

On July 28, my father's birthday, he sends an e-mail with no message. A word doc is attached: The correct title of the poem he sent is "When You Are Old" and the word "crown" in the last line should be "crowd." I did not reply:

When you are old and grey and full of sleep by W. B. Yeats

When you are old and grey and full of sleep,

And nodding by the fire, take down this book,

And slowly read and dream of the soft look

Your eyes had once, and of their shadows deep;

How many loved your moments of glad grace,

And loved your beauty, with love false or true,

But one man loved the pilgrim's soul in you,

And loved the sorrows of your changing face;

And bending down below the glowing bars,

Murmur, little sadly, how Love fled

And paced upon the mountains overhead

And hid his face amid a crown of stars. [crown should

be crowd.]

He appears outside at the Metro Center stop near my condo twice in September at the very time I arrive to take the line to GWU where I teach.

He attends my book club on two Tuesdays at Teaism in October. On the first, I am alarmed; on the second D., the man I used to call my husband, accompanies me.

I receive via e-mail his US Air Dividend Miles statements through December.

The last one: His Dividend Miles # I shall omit here:

Beginning balance	2,208
Miles deposited this period	684
Miles debited this period	0
Ending balance	2,892

Finally, nothing.

Headline, *The New York Times*: To Protect Ancient City, China Plans to Raze it: The city is Kashgar with 13,000 families. Fear of an earthquake is the official reason given.

On this oasis on the Old Silk Road, *The Times* (http://www.nytimes.com/2009/05/28/world/asia/28kashgar.html?_r=1&scp= 1&sq=Kashgar&st=cse) ran a black and white photo: Young girl on cobbled walled alley, in dance position, trousers covered by translucent dress, tied at the waist in back, the skirt swept in the triangle of movement, her scarf in mirrored swirl, her thin body balanced on athletic-shoed toes.

T.S. Eliot says,

> Do not let me hear
>
> Of the wisdom of old men, but rather of their folly,
>
> Their fear and frenzy, their fear of possession,
>
> Of belonging to another, or to others, or to God.
>
> The only wisdom we acquire
>
> Is the wisdom of humility: humility is endless.

Let me be clear: My husband was the earthquake. We were the body-balanced and *we* razed it.

> The houses are all gone under the sea.
>
> The dancers are all gone under the hill.

Exit Strategy

After the emergency egress from the psychiatrist, I wondered, Will I ever write again, love again, have sex again, come to orgasm again, be loved again, be safe again? It is spring and I think about the Kentucky Derby and the elusive hope for the Triple Crown. I saved this story Joe Drape filed for *The New York Times* on War Emblem, the 2002 Derby winner:

> War Emblem is in therapy.
> He is isolated from the other studs at Shadai Stallion Station in the hope that he will feel safe and more confident in his sexuality. Mares surround him in an effort to revive a long-dormant libido. (http://www.nytimes.com/2008/04/28/sports/othersports/28emble m.html)

I have spoken here too much about my husband's dormant libido.

Writing equals betrayal. In my search: Auden says, *There is always another story, there is more than meets the eye.* I seek syllogisms:

> all x and y
> z is x
> ∴

War Emblem at nine years old—How many man years or dog years is that?—and five and a half years in stud, in contact with hundreds of mares, has managed to mate with only 70 of them, which is half of most stallions' yearly output. He has not produced a live foal since 2005, and the last time it was confirmed that he ejaculated in the company of a mare was in 2006. He did it once.

> He was one of the quirkiest horses I've ever had," said the trainer Bob Baffert, who won his third Derby with War Emblem and pulled into the Belmont Stakes with a chance to sweep the Triple Crown. The big, black son of Our Emblem, however, stumbled at the gate and finished eighth.

Two strikes and you're out: I have two failed marriages.

> "He was real temperamental," Baffert said. "He did not like other horses or people that much. We used to joke that he may have had an unhappy childhood."

D., still the loner. That's the view from my vantage point: not able to stop loving, in seek of exit strategy.

Did you know that couples go into therapy to separate? D. refuses couples therapy.

Experts say,

> [T]his could be a case of juvenile bachelor stallion behavior.
>
> Dr. Sue McDonnell, a specialist in equine sexual behavior at the University of Pennsylvania's New Bolton Center, explained that in the natural setting of a herd, a dominant horse mates with the mares, while the other males stay in the background.
>
> "They become this little troupe of bachelors waiting for their own harem, but they're submissive to the top dog," McDonnell said. "They are immature and intimidated.
>
> "By separating him from other stallions, he has a chance to become more confident."

Syllogisms follow:

> Her mother called her "Mar."
> Mary's mother is dead.
> No one calls Mary "Mar."
> D. equals War Emblem.
> Mary equals Mare.
> Mary seeks emblem.

Mary stumbles at the gate.

Photo by Andy Duback (www.andyduback.com)

I'm Cooked

The chase begins again in earnest, on my part anyway, with another widower, an aerospace engineer, who some eight months before lost his wife to lung cancer (quick and pernicious and I don't think she smoked).

I believe in rescue. I mistyped that at first and wrote *rescure*, saw the word *cure* inside and wondered how crazy or crazed I am. I know we must rescue ourselves. You don't have to tell me that. But when our goose is cooked, don't we all want the guy on the white horse—even if the horse turns out to be stationary and turning on a merry-go-round? Where you might think I am at this point. And I'm with you.

So I read the paper: "Almost exactly two years after it embarked on the biggest financial rescue in American history, the Federal Reserve acknowledged that the economy," according to *The New York Times*, "was pulling out of its downward spiral and announced a step back toward normal policy."

I believe my downward spiral is ending. After all, it is August, the month the shrinks escape, gardens overgrow, and children turn off the TV to go buy school supplies.

I meet the second widower one Sunday morning on the Internet—let's call him m.r.s. (his initials and he, as you will see, is widowed but still married), profiled in Forbes, owns his company consults with the Pentagon but is not a

Republican, thank god, (yes, I googled him)—and we agree to meet for an early dinner at Matchbox, great pizza, near my condo. He flirts with me through IM: "You are a beautiful woman and write with both a comic touch and a real sense of romance/passion. It brings out the foolishness in us men. I like the Robert Browning line, 'Grow old with me, the best is yet to be.' "

Here is what he is referring to (Oh sure my photo from 2006—so I don't look that good now anyway)—and my Internet dating profile: see what *you* think:

I'm a fiction writer. I've returned from a visiting-writer gig at a major university in the Midwest. I am separated, have been for almost four years, live alone, own my own condo. I would like to talk with an intelligent man interested in the arts and who actually likes the part of my profile that begins: I'd give most anything to see Érik Bédard pitch against the Yankees. But then, of course that fact fits with these and, if you see what I mean, you may like to talk to me: I read literary fiction and poetry (Nabokov, Joyce, Wolfe, Roth, Bellow, Kunitz, Bishop, Lawrence and especially Auden); love the movies, anything and everything, think a great actor gives us a backstage pass to his soul; loved *Wild Strawberries, Match Point*, and *The Thomas Crown Affair* (the second version! —go figure? But Steve was great in the first one.)

The profile, by the way or not so by-the-way, I hide after m.r.s. I can't do this anymore and here's why:

m.r.s. hit me, the sight of him, like a ton of bricks. I was immediately smitten and then he spoke: He speaks of literature and Mother Teresa, he plays bridge, he had sex with his wife every day for thirty-five years, until she got sick, he thinks I am beautiful, he holds my hand when we cross the street, and I am a goner. He has been widowed for only six months. And, to this question that he actually asks on the first date, "Do you believe in beshert?"—*Meant-to-be* would be the loose translation of the Yiddish—I answer, "I do.

Remember in *Four Weddings and a Funeral* when Andie McDowell advises Hugh Grant on getting married? "It's pretty easy really," she says in the church at his wedding to Duckface. "Whenever someone asks you a question, answer 'I do.' "

I think a second chance (Okay call it a third if you are nitpicking about my two marriages) fortuitously walked into my life and a door I thought was forever closed opened. We neck impetuously on my couch and move to the bedroom with his pleadings. He says we must not make love—though he does want to—"but can't we take off some of our clothes and lie down together? You can do this," he says. I answer, "I can, but I'm old." He says, "You have the shape of an hourglass." Not true: I look like a small bosc pear. But it was the perfect response, time and shape in metaphor. He is a short (D. is so tall), gorgeous man—he and I are exactly the same age (D. is almost four years younger—perhaps that explains the wreckage?). m.r.s. is an Aries and I am a Pisces. Believe it or not, this aerospace engineer ends up telling me he was born on the cusp of Pisces (the twelfth and final sign of the Zodiac) and that he is ruled by Mars and Neptune. So, he says, we are a Neptune/Mars combination, on the cusp of rebirth, associated with the beginning of human life.

So, I cook the Thomas Keller chicken for him. At that dinner I serve the chicken, the roasted potatoes, carrots and shallots on my farm dishes, the naïf pattern by Villeroy and Boch. m.r.s. tells me he bought the full set for his wife when he was in Luxembourg where they are made. He is speechless before his dinner plate.

I am unglued. Like a school girl: Remember promise in giant red doors you saw while your knees shook at the edge of the playground with book bag and lunch pail, cold from the thermos of milk? The sound of the future in the creak of the bindings of black and white speckled notebooks? How hope smelled in the wood of sharp yellow pencils? Remember how long red margins ruled down the side of lined paper you titled "My Summer Vacation" and you learned at hard desks how to write—in narrow white spaces—of weather, and clothes, and long days at the beach instead of skies bursting color like peaches and plums or birds' feet on sand like the sweetness of time?

He calls the next day after the roasted chicken to say he is overwhelmed with guilt even though his wife is dead. He tells me he "feels badly." That he is attracted to me but that that is the problem. He tells me he did not mean to mislead. He tells me this before he explains the Gaussian concept in answer to a question I have about a scientific passage I am writing in my novel. I am hearing the message loud and clear: In short, he is not ready.

I am devastated, *again*. I write him:

> Dear m.,
>
> You may indeed feel bad that, for example, you were not able to

sleep over with someone you liked for complicated reasons that you could barely even explain (note the proper use of the adverb 'barely')—but you do need the adjective to describe this state of mind. However, if you were not able to touch her, you would appropriately say that you have lost your sense of touch; for example, I could not touch her because I feel badly; I can barely tell her skin from her teeth, without telling her of course that you wished to escape by the skin of your teeth (refer to Thorton Wilder for more on this last phrase.)

The reason for all this is that the verb *feel* when used to describe one's feelings does not take an adverb. That is because it is what as known as a 'linking verb,' much like the verb *to be*, and it takes what in grammar is known as a 'subject complement adjective.' But the verb, though it works like the verb *to be*, cannot be replaced with the verb *to be*.

Thus, the confusion among educated folk. A person who feels bad is very rarely, though could be, bad. As in the phrase: I am bad. Something none of us wants to be except in the bedroom, of course, where consenting adults may be as *bad* as they both think appropriate.

I write this note to you because I would feel bad if I had misled you as to the proper usage of a word to describe one's feelings.

Grammatically yours,

Mary

I call D. and tell him I think we truly need NOT see each other until after the agreement is signed. I tell him I am an all or nothin' girl and I can't bear what has happened. I have to find a way to live with what happened. I have to find a way to move on.

I do believe my heart is broken and that I am a fool. I call my daughter Sarah and tell her about m.r.s. She's been burned by both D. and m., the first widower, the psychiatrist, and now sees me as foolish, impulsive, inexplicably romantic and has begun not to answer my phone calls. She writes an e-mail in the morning instead of calling me back: "I heard the phone ring downstairs when I was asleep last night. This morning I saw it was you. Is everything okay? Sorry I didn't pick up. By the time I was awake enough to know the phone was ringing it had stopped."

"Did you see this article?" She includes a link to a site in Paris from our favorite newspaper *The New York Times* where now I am reading about the economic recovery that is not quite here—and ain't that an understatement. She says, "I think we should take cooking classes in Paris together. Wouldn't that be fun?" She and her husband Ryan and Lila, my grandchild, are going in September for six months: Sarah will have no time for cooking classes between the research for her next book and Lila. But she knows I need to recover and that I have planned to rent an apartment in Marais. I hope to write in a garret (another dream?) while the world goes south.

I find this at WIRED

(http://www.wired.com/techbiz/it/magazine/17-03/wp_quant) where Felix Salmon had said in February 2009,

> A year ago, it was hardly unthinkable that a math wizard like David X. Li might someday earn a Nobel Prize. After all, financial economists—even Wall Street quants—have received the Nobel in economics before, and Li's work on measuring risk has had more impact, more quickly, than previous Nobel Prize-winning contributions to the field . . . For five years, Li's formula, known as a Gaussian copula function, looked like an unambiguously positive breakthrough, a piece of financial technology that allowed hugely complex risks to be modeled with more ease and accuracy than ever before. With his brilliant spark of mathematical legerdemain, Li made it possible for traders to sell vast quantities of new securities, expanding financial markets to unimaginable levels . . . Li's Gaussian copula formula will go down in history as instrumental in causing the unfathomable losses that brought the world financial system to its knees.

> How could one formula pack such a devastating punch? The answer lies in the bond market, the multi-trillion-dollar system that allows pension funds, insurance companies, and hedge funds to lend trillions of dollars to companies, countries, and home buyers.

> A bond, of course, is just an IOU, a promise to pay back money with interest by certain dates . . .

> Bond investors are very comfortable with the concept of probability.

I ask you: What is the probability that my goose is cooked?

In the Grimm Fairy Tale "The Goose-Girl," a beautiful princess is betrayed and, instead of marrying her prince, must tend the geese while her talking horse Falada tries to save her even after his murder, after his head has been pinned to the wall. The princess is now the goose girl who, after driving the geese into the country, unravels her plaits of long golden hair that *shone with radiance*.

But Falada can save her because his head, nailed to the wall can reply when the goose-girl says, *Ah Falada, hanging there!*

Falada says and the prince's father learns of his reply: *Alas, young queen how ill you fare! If this your mother knew, her heart would break in two*.

Could it be that D. will ride a white horse? Or is he on the merry-go-round with me?

The real q.: How would Carl Friedrich Gauss measure the probabilities?

Double doors

This is the way one version of the story "The Frog-Prince" by the Grimm Brothers begins.

> The princess had a golden ball in her hand, which was her favourite plaything; and she was always tossing it up into the air, and catching it again as it fell. After a time she threw it up so high that she missed catching it as it fell; and the ball bounded away, and rolled along upon the ground, till at last it fell down into the spring. The princess looked into the spring after her ball, but it was very deep, so deep that she could not see the bottom of it. Then she began to bewail her loss, and said, 'Alas! if I could only get my ball again, I would give all my fine clothes and jewels, and everything that I have in the world.'
>
> Whilst she was speaking, a frog put its head out of the water, and said, 'Princess, why do you weep so bitterly?' 'Alas!' said she, 'what can you do for me, you nasty frog? My golden ball has fallen into the spring.' The frog said, 'I want not your pearls, and jewels, and fine clothes; but if you will love me, and let me live with you and eat from off your golden plate, and sleep upon your bed, I will bring you your ball again.' 'What nonsense,' thought the princess, 'this silly frog is talking! He can never even get out of the spring to visit me, though he may be able to get my ball for me, and therefore I will tell him he shall have what he asks.' So she said to the frog, 'Well, if you will bring me my ball, I will do all you ask.'

The only fairy tale couple I know about: Barack and Michelle. The charmed couple.

Remember when Barack was first elected and the two went abroad? Foreign policy and romance were on his mind. You could read about this in *The Daily Mail Online* of Britain and be reminded that Barack

- requested a romantic dinner with a view of Prague, where they can eat the best Czech food. "They have spent days trying to decide on the right restaurant," a source told *The Times*.
- It is thought the First Couple have chosen Hergetova Cihelna, or The Brick House, on the banks of the River Vlatava.
- The restaurant has views of Prague's most famous landmark, the Charles Bridge, for their romantic dinner.

I am separated from the man I *thought* was the other half of my fairy tale. I learn from him that he must have surgery—so-called *minor* surgery: a hernia—and needs a ride home. I don't have a car, so he picks me up at my condo on his way to Sibley Hospital so that I can drive him home after the surgery.

I faced double doors. D. had surgery on April 6 (I do not make this date up) at Sibley Hospital, where I met my father's corpse on June 6, 1996, on a gurney on linoleum floors behind a curtain in the emergency room.

An emergency.

D. and I and our daughter Sarah had gone to D.'s company picnic on Johnson Island. June 6, 1996. Yes, I see it too: 6-6-96. And the multiples of three and the terrifying to me: 666. It has taken more than a decade for me to recover from the shame (was it shame or regret?) of having gone to the picnic the day after my niece Wendy's wedding, the wedding my father could not attend because he lived in "assisted-living" he had so resisted. He was bent and frozen in the shape of a W after he'd fallen and broken his hip, after the Parkinson's disease that did not allow him to hop while the hip repaired, after he'd answered the surgeon's question as he lay on the gurney in another emergency room: "Mr. Tabor, tell me about your physical activity?" "I play tennis. Don't want to meet my slice."

Does a daughter argue with her father when he lies broken on a gurney? She should have.

He was eighty-two. He'd not played tennis for a decade. He'd played when he was young, stopped when he married, began again at fifty when he won a

Wilson racket in a raffle at a Metropolitan Life Insurance conference: he sold insurance door-to-door for thirty-eight years. He could beat both my husbands with that slice even when he could no longer run.

Watch them run.

But I do tell the surgeon when he asks, "Is there anything else we should know?" as we stand in the pre-op room before the surgery, that my father has an aneurysm at the base of his neck. For this reason the orthopedist says they will not use a local anesthetic. General anesthetic—out cold—must be used for fear of bursting the aneurysm with a spinal injection. General anesthesia and Sinemet, the drug my father is taking for the Parkinson's disease, and the disease itself do not mix. And my father comes out of the anesthesia with a form of schizophrenia that is treated without talking with me or his neurologist with a drug called Zyprexa that leaves my father more confused, placid, broken, bent.

Yes, I answered one question asked of me.

Did you know that orthopedists do not ask the question about, let us call it *tennis*—for after all the ball has fallen into the river and only the frog can retrieve it—of elderly women who have fallen? They fix their hips with cement and the women get up and walk the next day, maybe the same day. But a man who plays tennis: He gets repaired with a plate and a screw and must hop for six months until the hip heals. My father could not hop: the tremor in his legs.

More than a decade later I recall that day and the day I went to the picnic after I visited him at Manor Care Spring House on River Road, after I'd seen that he had a cold and I knew he might die: sedentary and confused. A cold becomes pneumonia.

Double doors do not mean the ball that the princess will attend with her prince. My sister or my mother or my father on a gurney went through double doors, pushed by attendants wearing colored caps and returned more broken than before.

On April 6, I kiss D. on the lips—I think, if I kiss him, . . .? I watch him go through the double doors with the doctor, with the anesthesiologist, with the nurse in colored cap, all in turquoise pajamas. I watch the doors close.

[T]he princess ran to the door and opened it, and there she saw the frog, whom she had quite forgotten. At this sight she was sadly frightened, and shutting the door as fast as she could came back to her seat. The king, her father, seeing that something had frightened

her, asked her what was the matter. 'There is a nasty frog,' said she, 'at the door, that lifted my ball for me out of the spring this morning: I told him that he should live with me here, thinking that he could never get out of the spring; but there he is at the door, and he wants to come in.'

D. recovers. He is well and strong. So am I. I have survived them all: my sister, my mother, my father: What do I deserve?

Did you know that in the Grimm fairy tale, the princess does not kiss the frog?

Send in the Clowns

I weep when famous people die: I cried when Audrey Hepburn died and bought stamps and pictures. I cried when Princess Di died and taped and watched the funeral and all the gory tabloid details. I'm a staunch Democrat and I cried when Ronald Reagan died and watched every second of his funeral. I'm Jewish and I wept when John Paul the II died, and followed not only the funeral but watched TV endlessly for white smoke to signal that a new pope had been named.

No one famous who matters to me has died today. I do not say this easily. It is Sunday. I live downtown next to St. Patrick's Church. As John Donne told us in Meditation XVII,

> No man is an island entire of itself; every man is a piece of the continent, a part of the main. If a clod be washed away by the sea, Europe is the less, as well as if a promontory were, as well as if the manor of thy friend's or of thine own were. Any man's death diminishes me, because I am involved in mankind, and therefore never send to know for whom the bell tolls. It tolls for thee.

When John Updike died, I read. First I wept, e-mailed my daughter and my former and much beloved student Sarah Krouse who were also, I learned, weeping. But I couldn't stop crying. I reread Updike because I have always it seems been reading him. He encourages me:

Yet, of course at each stage even in the narrowest passage, I had air to breathe, daily comforts and amusements, companions, and the blessed margin of unforeseeing that pads our adventure "here below"—a frequent phrase of my grandfather's, locating this world in relation to a better.

When my daughter was about to have her baby, my granddaughter Lila, I sat up in bed at 1 a.m. positive that she was in labor. While I sat upright, her call came—she *was* in labor. On the first flight out in the morning I flew to her side for this blesséd gift of life: a grandchild in my arms, my daughter Sarah in my arms, her husband Ryan in my arms. Perhaps my son would come from New York where he lives when he is not in Australia. My son Ben in my arms.

While I waited to fly, I slept: I went into the art room and on the blackboard is the drawing of the clowns and circus performers that I drew when I was a teenager and that I'd filled in with colored chalk, the skin nude, the costumes gold and red. What remains now is the outline of my drawing with no colors—amazing that it is still here in this room with so many years gone past. What I am assigned to do is to make a new drawing, but I am drawn solely to the outline on the board. All I want to do, all I *will* do is fill that in with any chalk I can find. I don't care about the assignment.

I have said here that I have wanted to shout, "Fire." I have slid the scenery panels of my life through backstage grooves while I've tried to kill myself off with binge smoking and drinking. But I am lousy at both it turns out. I get drunk fast and want to live. So I do neither—well, occasionally, I do both. Or, I am too much of a survivor. But one must not speak too soon.

While I wait for the bell to toll, the clown in the circus breaks through my transparent skin. My skin, the clown: beryl-blue like sapphire. Is the color of fire red? I think of the blue inside. I think green fire, white fire, black fire.

Maurice Blanchot says:

> The question concerning the disaster is part of the disaster: it is not an interrogation, but a prayer, an entreaty, a call for help. The disaster appeals to the disaster that the idea of salvation, of redemption might not yet be affirmed, and might, drifting debris, sustain fear.

> The disaster: inopportune.

Many years ago I stood with D. where he grew up and watched a fire. The heat was so incredibly hot that it reminded me of something I learned in physics: the fact that the air around a lightning bolt is hotter than the surface of the sun. It was a barn burning—not with any political or racial overtones, but a necessary burn of an old wooden grain bin in the center of town in Whiting, Iowa. It's a common enough event in rural parts of our country.

It was a controlled burn.

We were on the brink of disaster. The burn was not.

The disaster: bewitched.

The burn in Iowa didn't spread. It took place on a Saturday morning. Everyone in town knew about it. That's some six hundred people. And I suppose some of the surrounding townspeople had heard. The fire department burned the bin because it was no longer used. It had been in the center of town—the tallest building, about the height of a Washington office tower—for fifty or sixty years and held seed corn or soy beans. Wooden bins are rarely used now for this kind of storage.

The fire began inside the old bin. It burned from the inside out to keep it under control. Very quickly the entire structure was in flames but with a certain order—if anything can ever burn in an order—that made the walls fall in on themselves. The old buildings nearby were never in danger.

The firemen were so certain of their ability to control the fire that they allowed onlookers to stand, in my opinion, way too close—though I am forever glad to have been there with the heat in my face. The heat of this fire made me understand the power of lightning because the fire burned into me, into every part of me. Later, the ashes smoked and heated the air long past nightfall.

The space between us in our bed was a conflagration that neither of us could safely enter. That space was an uncontrolled fire. It is safety that is key to my analogy. One can create a conflagration in marriage or in betrayal of it. The controlled fire that burned the bin in D.'s home town makes my analogy clear. No one needed to be pulled from that fire. All were safe from it though in itself it was a burning danger. This is the difference between a controlled fire and a conflagration.

This is of interest to me and my penchant for the analytical, but it is hardly newsworthy as all of us who watch television or read the papers know.

So go ahead: Send in the clowns.

Or give me the end of the Grimm fairy tale "Brother and Sister":

And as soon as the bewitcher was burnt to ashes, the roebuck changed his shape, and received his human form again, so the sister and brother lived happily together all their lives.

PS: I Love You?

P.S. I Love You is a 2007 film with Gerard Butler and Hillary Swank, two actors I adore in a Rom-Com that is not worth analyzing, that I don't own, but that gave me pause. Sure Gerard Butler (also in *The Ugly Truth*: great title) stopped my heart but then so did Jeffrey Dean Morgan who closes the deal in the film.

P.S. I Love You relies on the death of the character Butler so effectively plays with wry intelligence and wit—not characteristic of the letters that drive the film—so a bit out of sync there. But *death and love* cause me to write a P.S. on **Let the Rom-Coms Roll.**

I revisit here that early relationship with the real estate developer m. because he revisited me over a year later well after he had been dating the woman in New York. I learned something about myself when I saw him again.

Before the ellipsis, before his silence, m. and I agreed that I would cook dinner for him. Perhaps, the cynic in me now says, he did this while he was already pursuing the woman in New York. This dinner-to-be was, of course, *before* he told me about her.

But it's hard to see through the lens of grief. *P.S. I Love You* fumbles sincerely to do that, a mighty task for the Rom-Com.

That night I prepared Mussels with Potatoes and Spinach, one of D.'s favorite dishes, and for the actual first time, I cooked, meaning I did not throw together a meal, but cooked with the right-tool-for-the-task verve in my condo's pared down kitchen.

I considered: No way I could I do this for D.

But I am doing it for m.! Does this mean I have come through?

Kitchens and men *are* all about love, despite what your stomach tells you.

Just as m. was to arrive and the deconstructed parts of this meal were about to come together, he called and canceled. His reason, so heartrending that love and death joined in my heart: His oldest daughter needed him. He had to go home. He was looking for love after the death of his wife. But it was her *mother* who had died. He wrote the next day and explained that his daughter had had a headache. I heard heartache. I wrote him this:

> Dear m.,
>
> You are good to write after also calling and explaining quite fully. I deeply respect your commitment and sensitivity to your children.
>
> I spent last night after your call (well, cooking) but also thinking about R.'s [his daughter's] bouts with grief—as I suspect that may be the less-spoken part of what goes on as she tries so hard to find her way, dunno, just a guess. I don't know her of course.
>
> Too soon, way too soon, your daughter has had to learn that death defines life. This next thought is for you (actually all of this e-mail is really for you): Take hope in the fact that, without a doubt, the wisest people I have known experienced adversity early in life. And what more could we want as we journey ourselves but to know that wisdom might in fact come to our children even as we struggle helplessly to protect them from adversity?
>
> Mary

m.'s silence followed, the girlfriend in New York, the reason, as he later explained.

When I met him a year later when he considered getting together again with me—or perhaps he needed something else that this time I could not give—I had wised up. But I was deeply saddened to learn that he'd dated this woman for over a year, that she had inexplicably dumped him, and that he could never forgive her for that. He actually said *never* in the same sentence with the indomitable *and I loved her.* She had lost her husband in the Twin Towers. How could *never* apply here?

We love on debt: *Carta di credito finito*?

Here's the recipe for the meal I ate alone:

Mussels with Potatoes and Spinach from *Gourmet's Five Ingredients* (a great little cookbook. Recipe, slightly adapted here)

(start to finish 35 minutes)

1 lb small red potatoes

3 T. olive oil

1 T. minced garlic (I use more)

2 lb mussels (preferably cultivated, meaning less gritty, cleaned and beards removed)

½ lb baby spinach (I use more)

1. Simmer potatoes in enough salted water to cover by 1 inch until tender, about 15 minutes. Drain under cold water. Pat dry; cut in half or quarters.

2. Heat two tablespoons of oil in a large heavy skillet (I use my cast iron pan) until hot but not smoking, then sauté potatoes with salt (I use Kosher coarse salt), turning as they brown (don't turn too often or potatoes will crumble instead of getting crisp—and that's what makes this dish great), about 10 minutes.

3. In a 5 to 6 quart pot, while potatoes are sautéing, cook garlic in one tablespoon of oil until fragrant (don't burn the garlic; burnt garlic ruins a dish). Stir in mussels and ¼ cup water (white wine also works, but I use a little more when I choose wine), cover pot and cook until mussels open (take them out as they open), about three to five minutes (discard unopened mussels).

4. Add spinach to the pan with the potatoes that are now crisp and toss until spinach wilts. Serve potatoes and spinach with mussels.

I used to put the spinach, potatoes and mussels together in the Italian ceramic bowl D. gave me, the bowl he now has in his apartment—it's on loan? Oh, how I fantasize!—the bowl that thrives with color (red, black, blue) and molded striped blue and white handles, the line *carta di credito* along the side in script.

In my Rom-Com-Life, I considered actually writing at the end of my e-mail to m. about death and love and wisdom, "P.S.: I think I could love you" and thought better of it, but in my fantasy cinema you'd have seen me write it, delete it, and you would have known.

But then, I wised up. And life is not a Rom-Com.

PS: When is the *carta di credito finito?*

Square the Circle?

Heard on the street: "If you can't solve the problem, prolonging it will make money."

Read in *The New York Times*:

> In the latest installation of the soap opera gripping Italy, Prime Minister Silvio Berlusconi, 72, on Monday demanded an apology from wife, Veronica Lario, 52, a day after she told Italian newspapers that she wanted a divorce. Mr. Berlusconi said he did not think the couple could reconcile. 'I don't think so. I don't know if I want it this time,' Mr. Berlusconi said in an interview that appeared Monday in the leading Italian newspaper, Corriere della Sera, 'Veronica will have to publicly apologize to me. And I don't know if that will be enough.' In recent days, Ms. Lario has criticized her husband for cavorting with younger women and for his center-right coalition's plans to nominate a slate of attractive women to run for the European Parliament.
>
> World Briefing, Rachel Donadio, *The New York Times*, Tuesday, May 5, 2009.

Read in *The New York Times*: Alessandra Stanley, the television critic, commented on John and Elizabeth Edwards:

> Mrs. Edwards star turn on 'Oprah' doesn't quite fit the template of naïve New World idealism; it looked more like an exquisite form of revenge, the kind of well-oiled comeuppance that Marquise de Merteuil concocted in "Dangerous Liaisons."

"More Than One Way to Skin a Cad," Alessandra Stanley, Week in Review, "Critics Notebook," *The New York Times*, Sunday, May 10, 2009

Read in The New York Times Magazine:

The diagnosis was staring her in the face for years, but she did not see it. Psychologists call this inattention *blindness*—instances when we don't see something because it's not what we are expecting to see; it's not what we are looking for. Sherlock Holmes has a somewhat different description. "I trained myself to notice what I see," Holmes says. Arthur Conan Doyle, himself a physician, imbued his character with the kind of keen observational skills so essential to a good physician. This ability consists of casting a wide net to see the whole picture—even when the complaint that brings the patient to medical attention is commonplace, like insomnia.

"Sleepless," by Lisa Sanders, M.D., *The New York Times Magazine,* May 10, 2009.

These headlines in my mind.

I roast a chicken, alone, on a Sunday and hold in memory the dinners I laid down on our mahogany table with its gold inlaid border that had begun to show the table's age—now gone—like all the Sunday dinners, the weeks and months and years, in soups I had simmered, made fragrant with carrots and onions, bay leaf and peppercorns, in roasts I had crusted with pepper and salt, with leaves of rosemary grown in my garden—now gone—in buttery pie crusts I had rolled on my marble board in the kitchen—I still have the board but no room to lay it down—filled with blackberries from the bushes by my fence—gone—sprinkled with sugar and covered with strips of dough woven over and under each other like our lives.

Is what I do in these pages *revenge*? I worry this thought. Meanwhile the headlines point me like a compass that tries to square the circle:

Prolong the problem.

Demand apology.

Humiliate spouse.

Or analyze: In her book *Dreams of Love and Fateful Attractions,* psychiatrist Ethel Spector Person notes,

Many tentative forays into love are aborted either because they pose real or symbolic threats to selfhood. Even when the integrity of the self is not at risk as it is in enslavement, pride, and self-esteem may be (or appear to be) endangered. The love may become frightened at the strength of his impulse toward surrender and the lack of autonomy he thinks it implies and he may make strenuous efforts to disengage. Or, out of self-protectiveness, he may pick an Other who does not reciprocate his feeling, and consequently, one who sets external limits to his attempt to merge. Fearing merger, he thus sets up a situation which will prevent it. Similar motives dictate the behavior of the lover who after moments of great intimacy, particularly sexual moments, reasserts his separateness by withdrawal or by starting a quarrel. The more soulful and intimate the love-making, the greater the dread of loss of self, of dissolution (or emptiness) afterwards, and the sadness or distancing that surfaces in response to that dread.

Or see: Two children have figured out how to dance, a performance. They are in a hospital (A lifetime of hospitals lie in my childhood and adulthood. Two hospitals more recently: D.'s hernia operation in D.C. and the birth of my grandchild in Chicago.) There is an elevator in the hospital and the doors to the elevator open onto the children, a boy and a girl, who are on the bed. The performance, the dance—had they been rehearsing?—was going to be at eleven in the morning. A third person, the observer who catches them at the dance in an inappropriate place, wants to help them, protect them. She watches the dance, a ballet: the boy lifts the girl who is on point. The angle of her body defies. Why, before he lifts her, while she stood on one toe, while she extended her leg back, her arm forward, did she not fall?

The observer knows this: If you can't solve the problem, look. Do not try to square the circle. The circle will square itself.

Pull Out the Map

So after the real estate developer/widower m., after the widower who is still married m.r.s., after the psychiatrist, I am devastated and freed.

Did you know that Greenland was once ruled by Denmark? I read this in *The New York Times* where I learned of Greenland's independence. I wondered what exactly Denmark has been doing with Greenland. I learned there may be oil reserves there and this holds some interest for me as I used to work for the oil industry. And Denmark, being who Denmark is, will let those oil reserves go because I am hoping: Some things are more important than money.

I worked for the oil industry? Square peg in round hole who managed to fit. Oh, the paradoxes abound.

Was this how I managed to fit inside my marriage?

I wonder what Greenlanders feel. I learn that that they like me have concerns about their name, their emblem. Their real name is their Inuit name: Naalakkersuisut—"the first time in history, officials said, that word had been used in a Danish government document." This was the day that declared some sort of gradual independence for Greenland. What exactly is *gradual independence.* You're either independent or you're not. I can hear my father saying this. I was talking about assisted living and he said, "You're either living or you're not." His, a much better line. I am working on living fully.

I am reading about Greenland in, of course, *The New York Times.* My young friend Sarah Krouse with whom I went to see the chick-flick *The Proposal* tells me at lunch that maybe I could love *The NYT* a bit *more*, meaning, of course, that I love the paper too much, refer to the paper too often.

I think about this. After all, I start my morning with that paper even though I am not from New York. I am from Baltimore and, I fear, I don't long for that paper though I used to read it regularly. But who owns that paper now?

Who owns whom? That is the question.

Let's talk about *The Proposal.* A chick-flick about what we all supposedly want: we people who were not meant to ever fall in love and marry and who do. This movie steals during opening bits from three other movies I actually like better: *The Devil Wears Prada*: Margaret, aka Sandra Bullock, is a witch on her broom much like Meryl Streep playing some version of Dianna Vreeland. Greencard: Margaret is about to be deported to Canada like Gérard Depardieu who is about to be deported to France—now how can that be a fate worse than death? This also reminds me of *French Kiss* where Meg Ryan is about to be deported *from* Canada to the United States while she is in search of her belovèd Charlie who left her—she has lost her passport along with other complications while she is *in* France where she will live happily ever after. And by the end, *The Proposal* steals from a fourth I like better: *While You Were Sleeping:* Here too the Sandra Bullock character has no family; both her parents are dead; she is an only child. She allows misunderstandings to pile up while a family adopts her.

The *Proposal* has a heart all its own in Alaska of all places (Is that near Greenland?) and though this chick-flick did not bring me to tears . . . Well, actually there was a moment for me when Bullock tells about getting her tattoo after her parents had died. Something about that revelation was so bare—and her delivery. I do love Sandra Bullock.

After all, I have lost both my parents and my sister. And there was little help from D.'s family while the devastation of my immediate family proceeded like an inexorable glacier—only faster. His parents are not affectionate and don't believe that death, separation, or god-no-divorce should be discussed. They don't embrace. Have you ever experienced the spider hug? D. was not like them but was. Paradoxes abound.

He is in search of his map. D. is from Iowa. When my Uncle Dave first met him, he insisted that D. was from Ohio or Idaho. He had never heard of Iowa. He demanded, "Get me a map!"

So I'm obsessed with *The New York Times.*

Oh, you don't think that follows? I used to start my morning with D.—actually, I used to wake up with D. Big difference. I actually have to go get *The New York Times.* I don't roll over and see it or roll over and into its folds. You can do that with a man you love: fold into him with no worry about what is above or below the fold or where the sheets are.

The Greenland story is below the fold.

Yesterday, I lay on the National Mall—the nation's front yard is my backyard; I can walk there in less than ten minutes from my book-lined condo that was so hard-earned after D. left me. I saw clouds like shaken-out sheets on a blue sky.

Greenlanders must feel like D.: They don't think anyone knows where they are. They pull out maps to prove their existence.

What, dear reader, do you think this is? Have you seen the movie *Off the Map?* Not a chick-flick: a heartbreaker. Netflix it.

Looking for the Map

Jenny Sanford, wife of the governor of South Carolina, was quoted in my favorite rag *The New York Times*, as she ended her foray with reporters obsessed with her husband's admitted affair with an Argentine woman, "I wish we had room on the boat for all of you, but we do not." She was about to go on a trip, in the middle of the sea, to, presumably, get away from the media storm.

She appeared to know where she was going, but I think somewhere along the line, she will need a map.

D., while looking for his map, told me that he had built his boat. How many divorced men do you know who live in Annapolis and have bought a boat? D. has built a metaphorical boat. He wants to have dinner. He wants to go to a movie with me. Does he want to be with me? Hard to tell.

He tells me he needs to figure out how to sail it. He tells me if I wait, the boat will be there. There will be room on that boat for me.

The waiting is hard so he tells jokes:

A genie appears before an old Jew and offers him one wish—anything he wants. The old man strokes his beard, thinks for a minute and says, "Wait a minute let me get my map." He brings out an old, wrinkled map of the Middle East, spreads it out before the genie and tells him, "See these countries here? They don't get along. They have fought for thousands of years. I would like to see them all live together in peace." The genie looks slightly taken aback. He says, "I've heard of this. I don't think what you want is at all possible, even for me. Is there anything else—anything—that you would like instead?" A wistful smile crosses the old man's face as he says, "Well, I'd like my wife to give me a blowjob." After a long pause, the genie replies, "Can I see that map again?"

The elephant on the table sits in this joke.

When we were together, he could not tell me why pleasure was problematic. And I could not forgive him for not taking pleasure when I offered it. I am ashamed of this now—among many other things that sit in the shame box of the map I need. The shame box sits with the north, south, east, west compass. No way to find my way without it.

One Valentine's day, I waited at home for him in the four-story house in Adams Morgan with the chef's kitchen. I finished my writing and then made his favorite dish: Russian Chicken Burgers with Stroganoff Sauce. I roasted beets in the oven (if you haven't done this, it's worth a try: a roasted beet beats any beet you've ever eaten). I let them cool and then sliced the beets and cut the slices with a heart shaped cookie cutter (It was tacky, but I'd been shooting hoops for too long). I cooked rice: the Stroganoff sauce loves rice. I set the table with the farm dishes I love: scenes of home and family like the drawing my daughter made in first grade of a cutout butterfly pasted and floating on background of scribbled chalk—sun, grass, house (right in the center)—now on faded construction paper. This childhood drawing hangs framed in the condo where I live alone now. It used to hang in my writer's room and library in the four-story house where that Valentine's Day dinner went south when I went south. We had eaten in the dining room and I came around the table to give him a blowjob: he shoved me away.

The shame of this is mine: I could not forgive him for this rejection. I don't understand even now why he couldn't accept, but I do understand how painful it must have been for him to push me away.

Salman Akhtar, psychiatrist and poet, has written in his book *Broken Structures*, "The Parable of Two Flower Vases." I hope he will forgive me here for paraphrasing the psychoanalytic phrasing of the question that resulted in his parable. The question was from a student who wanted to know (my version here) if someone who had lost his map and gone through the discovery needed to find it were compared with "a person who has always been psychologically well adjusted" would the two be indistinguishable?

Here is his answer:

Well let us suppose that there are two flower vases made of fine china. Both are intricately carved and of comparable value, elegance, and beauty. Then a wind blows and one of them falls from its stand, and is broken into pieces. An expert from a distant land is called. Painstakingly, step by step, the expert glues the pieces back together. Soon the broken vase is intact again, can hold water without leaking, is unblemished to all who see it. The lines along which it had broken, a subtle reminder of yesterday, will always remain discernible to an experienced eye. However, it will have a certain wisdom since it knows something that the vase that has never been broken does not: it knows what it is to break and what it is to come together.

Russian Chicken Burgers with Stroganoff Sauce: recipe by my beloved Pierre Franey who used to write the column "The 60-Minute Gourmet" in *The New York Times* where I found this:

The Burgers
1 ½ lbs. skinless and boneless chicken breasts
1 cup fine soft bread crumbs
1 ⅓ cup heavy cream
pinch cayenne pepper
⅛ tsp grated nutmeg
salt and freshly ground pepper
2 tablespoons corn or peanut oil (I use olive oil)
fresh dill for garnish

1. Cut the meat (remove cartilage) in 1-inch cubes and put in a food processor; blend to coarse texture.

2. In a mixing bowl, place meat. Blend ½ cup of the bread crumbs with the cream and add to meat. Add the cayenne, nutmeg, salt and pepper. Blend with hands.

3. Divide mixture into four balls, pat down to flatten, roll in bread crumbs. Press to make sure crumbs adhere.

4. Heat oil in a skillet. Cook the patties until browned on one side. Turn and cook 10 minutes on other side.

Stroganoff Sauce
1 tablespoon butter
¼ cup finely chopped onions
½ teaspoon paprika
1 tablespoon red wine vinegar
¼ teaspoon dried thyme
⅓ cup heavy cream

¼ cup sour cream

salt and freshly ground pepper

1. Melt the butter in a saucepan, add onion and paprika, Cook, stirring until the onion is wilted.

2. Add the vinegar and thyme. Cook stirring until the vinegar reduces.

3. Add the cream and cook until mixture reduces to about half.

4. Add the sour cream, salt and pepper. Heat to boiling point.

I am not able to make this dish in my condo. I am looking for my map and I don't have a boat.

So what do I do? I date. I screw around trying to find out if I am desirable. I think that is the problem.

D. tells jokes. Special bonus joke:

What do you get when you cross a genius and a hooker?

Answer: a fuckin' know-it-all.

Get me a map.

The Elephant

It's as if I have a large table with all the pieces for the jigsaw puzzle. It's a question now of seeing how they all fit. And what about the elephant? He's there, too.

Let Sotomayor Be the Judge

When Judge Sotomayor was about to be confirmed to the Supreme Court, I was more interested in her love life. She lives alone now. *The New York Times* told me that some time ago, after her divorce (she married young), she

> had fallen in love with the dapper and gray-bearded Peter White, a building contractor and that by 1998, they were engaged and living together, though they put off a wedding until after her Senate confirmation [to the Court of Appeals]. Her induction speech turned unexpectedly moving when she spoke of him.
>
> "Peter," she said, turning to her fiancé at the time, "you have made me a whole person, filling not just the voids of emptiness that existed before you, but making me a better, a more loving and a more generous person."
>
> "Many of my closest friends," she added, "forget just how emotionally withdrawn I was before I met you."
>
> With that, Mr. White helped her slip into a black appellate robe.
>
> Less than two years later, she gave a party at their newly renovated apartment for his 50th birthday. And not long after that, their relationship ended. He returned to Westchester County, bought a small boat and married a woman who was an acquaintance of the judge and 14 years her junior.

Bought a boat? Gimme a break.

Let Sotomayor be the judge:

Nietzsche asks, *Can you give yourself your own evil and your own good and hang your own will over yourself as a law? Can you be your own judge and avenger of your law? Terrible it is to be alone with the judge and avenger of one's own law. Thus is a star thrown out into the void and into the icy breath of solitude.*

. . . There are feelings which want to kill the lonely; and if they do not succeed, well, then they themselves must die. But are you capable of this—to be a murderer?

It took more than three years for my separation agreement to be signed. I don't fully understand the delay as not much money was at stake, and I *did* want it signed. D. says he did too, but I think the agreement presented a finality that I needed and he didn't. I could be wrong. Ultimately, he saw that signing it would help me to believe in him—and it did.

At first while it was unsigned—even though we lived apart—I feared dating or, as it turns out, screwing around because I feared angering D. and because I believed if I were not legally separated, I committed adultery. That may in fact be true, based on the ten commandments, a pretty good source. Do we read them literally? Thou shalt not kill. Thou shalt not commit adultery. Honor thy father and mother.

Nietzsche says, *The worst enemy you can encounter will always be you, yourself; you lie in wait for yourself in caves and woods.*

The first man I had sex with after D. left me was married and I knew it from the get-go. He knew me from my lecture work at the Smithsonian—took one of my classes there. I now wonder if I was giving off light the way a firefly flashes for sex. He would assert that some of the females eat the males.

a. wrote down for me all the reasons I should not sleep with him. He was seeking a long-term, casual affair in the city: my new condo would be convenient. You've got to admire the honesty of what he told me:

"Things a man seeking an affair but wishing to be honest might say. He would entitle this *Love's Labour's Lost*:

You do not want to be involved with someone like me. I could give you the Letterman 10 reasons but you don't need that many. Did you know that I am:

The grand wizard of the order of remorseless philanderers

A love sucking leach

One who likes to toy with women and words

An emotional and melancholy romantic

One who loves love

Emotionally needy

Unfaithful

Surely that is more than enough to make any sane woman avoid me like the plague."

And a. told me he had a long-term girlfriend whom he loved but couldn't see anymore because he was ruining her life. He lives in D.C. She lives in one of those New England states: Vermont or New Hampshire or Maine where he bought some real estate that he, on occasion, "must manage on-site."

He buys and sells large apartments, including tenements, and office buildings—this career after a long distinguished career in one of the sciences (vague on purpose here).

He pursued relentlessly once he knew "my story," as if *I* knew "my story." But I was good at the poor-little-me-husband-rejects-me story when a. invited me to lunch.

And I had all that La Perla underwear. And I owned a condo in D.C. I never let real-estate-guy into it. Instead I did this:

I had unexpected—not excused—sex with him in a building he owned that was being changed over, for a new renter, offices being readied. He had taken me to lunch and said before he dropped me at the metro, might he make a quick stop? Come along. While he stood evaluating the progress of the renovation, he said he'd take me to his club (there are such clubs in D.C., once called men's clubs: Who knew?) on Monday after the weekend that he'd spend with his wife, that he'd take me there in the late afternoon, to an elegant room where he would meet me again the next morning. It seemed so civilized, so genteel, so considerate, his proposal, his mannerly adultery. That's how it would be he said in the stripped-down office where we stripped down.

I removed my shirt after he kissed me. I removed my shoes and socks and trousers. My feet stuck to the floor because it had been treated with something that is done to floors before the final flooring is laid. He removed my panties that I'd chosen special to go with the bra even though they didn't match. I wore the bra with the tiny pink ribbons, one on the edge of each strap, the black bra with pink-stitched quilting across my breasts. My panties were sheer pale cream with a scalloped edge of embroidered flowers. The flowers, rimmed with green embroidered leaves, were the same shade of pink as the tiny ribbons, so tiny one would think a fairy or an angel child had tied them. I thought, Angel fingers on my chest, where the thin black straps lay, where the ribbon barely touched my skin. I thought this some time after I'd gone into the ladies room to tidy up and to clean the bottoms of my shoes which were covered with the sticky stuff. At home I washed my feet because they were also covered with the pale cream residue of the floor that had lain under the wood-brown Formica table where I'd lain while he'd stood and fucked me.

And someone saw us. The renter perhaps? Whoever the suited man was, he walked away. But his shadow remains on the inside of my eyelids.

I sat alone that weekend while a. and his wife went out with friends and knew that my father was right, when D. and I were still together, when my father lay in a state of anesthesia-induced schizophrenia after his hip had broken and been repaired, when he said, "You're a whore."

I refuse real-estate-guy. The Formica table and the dirt on the soles of my feet.

Real-estate-guy responds: "Mary, you are a ball buster!! I need to see a crack in your armour my dear sweet lovely lady—I think." Was the "I think" a comment on what he needed or on the question of my sweetness?

Later he pursued on issues of faith? I never understood. Catholics help me with this one. a. said, "I need to convert you to a Catholic for whom hope and faith are enduring."

He wrote: "Tomorrow is Lent and I will abstain until Easter the most wonderful holy day in Christendom." What was he abstaining from? Visiting the girlfriend in Vermont or New Hampshire? She was Catholic. That he'd told me. A single mother who worked two jobs: social worker and hotel housekeeper (how he met her: she carried his bags) and who raised one child, a daughter, alone.

During Lent, my separation agreement was finally signed. During Lent, I had lunch at Zaytinya, a tapas restaurant I love, with real-estate-guy a., who asked, "So, is your agreement signed?" And I answered, "Yes." "Well then," he said, "let's go to your condo." I replied that D. and I were seeing one another.

I have begun accepting dinner invitations, a movie and dinner invitations. Sometimes strained, sometimes strange but familiar like dreaming.

a. said, "The only reason he would ever get back with you is to avoid paying you alimony." I asked about the girlfriend. He told me that when her daughter had gone to college, she'd gone to an Ashram in India and when she returned, she broke off the affair for good.

That night I slept and dreamt: Heavy woman on road in Vermont, North Conway. She is outside and so is her refrigerator. My mother appears in the dream, leaves me to talk with the woman who tells her/me? that she must address the problem and the problem is that there is no sex in her marriage. So, I go with my mother to solve the problem. She and my father visit a whore. The bordello is across the street from a school in the middle of suburbia. The whore gives us each a set of picture frames with family pictures that are not our own; each of us has a picture of ourselves inside another family. The frames of the pictures are red. The whore dances with my father. I cannot bear to watch and take my pictures and leave. My mother finds me and tells me that all is well. I ask, How did that happen? She says, The whore danced with me. You can live here with us in this beautiful house.

Nineteen years ago my mother lay stroke-stricken and dying on the hospital bed where I'd come to see her in the part of the hospital where the dying are left to die. She was asleep and would die the next morning. The sheet was off, her nightgown, up around her waist, her hand on her clitoris. I covered her with the sheet. The memory lies on the insides of my eyelids.

If Nietzsche is right that we must murder the feelings that want to kill the lonely, I had not begun that conversation with myself. I had murdered my body instead.

Meanwhile D. tells me over dinner that he reads fiction in the solitude of his condo. I ask, "Why fiction?" He mumbles something about learning stuff. D. is a scientist and a financial guy. I want to know who he's reading. He talks of Tom McGuane, José Saramago. He says he's reading my unpublished novel. He says, "What you know. I want that." I'm not sure what he means or what this has to do with me. I'm confused and moved.

Does he want me? I don't ask that.

Let Sotomayor be the judge.

Let the Chase Begin

"So Who Owns Chrysler Now?" *Time Magazine* asked. Fiat owns Chrysler, or at least 35 percent of it, when that article was published, with an option to raise its share to 55 percent.

Detroit rethinks. The merger of Chrysler and Fiat occurs in June, the bridal month.

Mary rethinks: An Italian owns the Plymouth?

In the Grimm Brothers' story, "The Wedding and the Fox," the brothers include two stories to tell the tale. This choice may have been the brothers' academic-like reporting of the tales they "collected," but I am struck by the choice of two endings, as if both were possible, as if we had a choice. In the first, old Mr. Fox with nine tails plays dead because *he believed that his wife was not faithful to him and wished to put her to the test.* In the second story, the old fox *is* dead.

D. and I would have been married twenty-five years September 2009. "Which would you rather have?" I once asked D. "A Plymouth or an armchair, a comfortable, elegant armchair." "That depends," D. said, "on whether I needed to go to the grocery story or I was having the groceries brought in." I don't know if he knows that I used to think of him as a Plymouth: reliable, steady, made in America. I used to think of myself as the armchair.

During the time of separation I have had to think of D. as two stories: dead to me or playing dead.

You may think me a fool. Maimonides says, *Fools die for want of heart.*

In the first Grimm story, many suitors come but Mrs. Fox will only entertain the fox,

> who had nine tails like old Mr. Fox. But just as the wedding was going to be solemnized, old Mr. Fox stirred under the bench, and cudgeled all the rabble, and drove them and Mrs. Fox out of the house.

But I think she has been true to him. What could old Mr. Fox have been thinking?

Shortly before my stay in Missouri was to end, a pit bull attacked me. The guy across the street owned the dog but was house-bound due to his house arrest and the ankle bracelet that kept him there when the dog charged me as I got out of my 1998 used Ford Contour to enter the pit where I lived. A storm door saved me when I managed to get it between me and my attacker. Inside I stood shaking, once I'd gotten my front door closed, and I thought: still alive after all these years and despite these facts: No separation agreement, not even close then, still in love with the man who wrecked my life and no path to remaking it before me. But alive.

All this makes me think of the Dodge Charger R/T 440 Magnum, maybe the muscle car of my time, meaning movie-time, meaning *Bullitt*: Steve McQueen is detective Frank Bullitt, in case you don't remember. Bullitt in that dark green Ford GT Mustang 390 Fastback plays a tough cop in the car chase of all car chases. McQueen chases over the streets of San Francisco and the outlying highway the black Dodge Charger.

The Dodge Charger is D.'s dream car. I went to New York to have lunch with my son Ben and learned he'd bought a Dodge Charger R/T 440 Magnum. It's in Australia.

My son does not approve of the door I have opened to D.—the dinner dates and movies, the talking on the phone. "What are you doing?" he asks.

Ben thinks of D. as a pit bull. He thinks of my metaphorical storm door as inappropriately opened and my separation agreement as the assurance that I will be safe. After the pit bull attacked—many of these dogs in Oz so my son knows them well—"Anyone could outrun you," Ben said. "And that dog can outrun anyone." Ben suggested first that I move (with twenty-two days left on my lease?) and then that I park the car as near the storm door as I could.

I have parked my metaphorical car as near the storm door as I can. Perhaps D. is playing dead. Perhaps once the chase had begun—as indeed it has—he will pursue the way McQueen relentlessly pursues the truth in *Bullitt* because ultimately McQueen's chase is not for the Charger but for the real story: He makes sure that the dead Ross, whom he's been protecting, is thought to be alive: in a sense playing dead when he in fact is dead? so that Frank can get to the story in spite of Senator Chalmers, so that he can pursue the other story.

What do I know?

Nothing is what it seems. The Spy Museum near my condo in the Penn Quarter D.C. puts this line on signs in the Metro.

In a slim little book entitled *The Middle Passage* the Jungian analyst James Hollis advises: "What is not conscious from our past will infiltrate our present and determine our future. The degree to which we felt nurtured directly affects our ability to nurture others. The degree to which we feel empowered directly affects our ability to lead our own lives. The degree to which we can risk relationship . . ." depends.

D., when I met him, seduced me with a 1980 Fiat Spider 2000, otherwise known between us as "The Little Jewel." While I stood in the cold, waiting for the bus that would take me to the Metro that would take me to the job where I had met D., he would sometimes drive by and swoop me up: me in my overstuffed quilted red coat, my three bags—briefcase, purse and gym bag—and give me a ride to the Metro. He went out of his way to do this, knew when I would be standing there, knew how cold it was with two kids in elementary school and barely enough child support and salary to support them.

And so I married him: the first ending of my story. But why I married him lies inside. How do I explain?

When I had left my children's father, my daughter Sarah, six years old, said, "Can I tell you about my dream, Mommy? I dreamed of a present. It was big but, when I opened it, I found another box and inside that another one. I couldn't find the gift no matter how many I opened." We were driving with my father on a mundane errand. I can't now remember what it was—perhaps to get a toaster after the children and I moved from the giant of a house in Potomac that their father kept to the tiny rented house in Garrett Park Estates.

I think now again of Sarah who long ago sat on my lap and talked of opening boxes and knew with the wisdom of a child that it was not the gift that mattered.

It was not the house that mattered. When I married D., I knew that the heart—not the mind—is the seat of the brain. I could *see* his heart before he disappeared.

Perhaps the Grimm Brothers' second story's ending of "The Wedding of Mrs. Fox" might as easily be the ending of the first story: *and there was much rejoicing and dancing; and if they have not left off still, they are still dancing.*

Behind Chrysler is Fiat: Detroit rethinks.

Mary rethinks: Perhaps the Plymouth is a Fiat.

The Wave

The dream couple, Barack and Michelle, vacation in Martha's Vineyard or Hawaii: Ten-year-old Malia's head has sprouted almost above her father's shoulder—she is tall and willowy, feminine like her mother, lithe like her father. In a photo, gorgeous Michelle followed behind the two with her arm around Sasha: all the "girls" wore shades as Barack waved from the tarmack at the camera.

He did not wave as he boarded the helicopter on a trip to fly with his family to Camp David while health care reform and the war in Afghanistan loomed. He is, or at least I infer, burdened by the weight of reality.

But I recall his wave.

I recall my sister's wave before she got on the plane to Ethiopia, willowy at seventeen, three days before her eighteenth birthday that she would celebrate on her arrival and where she would marry. Her fiancé was in the Army on the base—gone!—in Eritrea. Thirty-five years later she would die on a gurney, legless and about to lose her arms because the blood from her heart could no longer reach her hands, blue with loss and the diabetes that took her life in 1993.

Her wave, full of hope and risk—that fearless wave. I write a postcard to her now: Wish you were here.

Trite but true.

How do I deal with all the leavings?

How do I deal with the desperate longing for a new beginning?

How do I deal with the shame of Internet dating that resulted in my daughter's assertion, "You are fickle, your fickle ways," said in merited disgust. "You have been in love and out of love." She recounts: "The psychiatrist who one day is the love of your life and the next, dangerous to your life. The college professor who one day is the love of your life and the next . . ." Need she or I go on reporting how I failed? How she must wonder, I suspect: Who is this woman I have called my mother?

Obama and Michelle remain the prince and princess in my tale of woe. But the Obama in real life took what some say was way too long to get the appointees of his administration in place.

Who are the appointees in my real life?

D., ephemeral?

I spent another Saturday night with him and I wrote him on Sunday morning:

> D.,
>
> It's hard for me on leaving you, as you could see yesterday. Sometimes, as over this weekend, it is also hard for me to be with you. I think that is because you are not yet able to be fully with me, to express the "need" to be with me in some way that makes sense to me, to put words and gestures around the need. You did seem to do that Saturday when you came over to me, when you sort of asked to stay, when you most poignantly laid your head on my chest. I needed to be cautious because if you had stayed, I would have given myself to you body and soul. That is what I want to do, need to do because I love you, flawed as I am, flawed as you are.
>
> I sense that I must take on—but you point out when I say this, "unfairly to yourself"—the blame for what seems lacking, something nameless, something I think, must be my fault and that needs to be "named." That doesn't mean I need to "understand" or have full disclosure about your journey toward your self, or in any way invade your privacy, but something seems withheld, almost as if to accept comfort from me would be to accept blame on *your* part. I am to blame. I *must* be. And I don't want you to take on my blame or *yours* with the stuff (talking, touching) that would help us *both*.
>
> M.

D. replies:

I have held back, I think, because I tend to see our relationship as "all or nothing." That my approach to you in any measured way would mean or be interpreted as full engagement—and be found lacking, because it is not yet full engagement. I have tended to be silent to protect that space I need to work through my personal past for a while [what does he mean by that? for what is between us is *personal*. Don't we share the past?], but I hear from you that, if I am present, you can also be present and help without full engagement. I do know what full engagement means and looks like, and I don't want you to think that I want something short of that. I am trying to get to the point of full engagement, and need some space—not totally—still to get there. I tend not to talk about that because I think it's hurtful to you, even though it has nothing to do with you and is not a rejection of you.

D.

I slept and dreamt after D. left me on Saturday night. I suppose this is one of those classic dreams like the airplane dream:

I am driving a big dark grey car—not like my father's Chevy, not a big rectangle, how I always thought of that bulky car he loved. I'm driving a hyperbolic bullet, sleek and large, probably a Toyota on a road that is soon covered with snow. I tell myself to slow down on this surface but can't keep my pedal off the metal. The snow is filling up my side windows and the rear window so that all I can see is forward. I know this is not a safe way to drive but I keep going though I don't know where I am going except that I am on Route 66. As the snow begins to fly off my peripheral windows and my vision opens up, I realize that I have passed a store at a mall where I am trying to meet my parents and my sister. My sister waves from an unknown location. I know I need directions.

I know my parents and my sister are dead. This thought is always a sad thought, sadder now that my husband has left me. When they died, I mourned their loss but had a sense of safety in my marriage. Now that is lost. My loneliness is profound, not unique, but profound.

I must stop the car and get directions. When I do, I discover—the way dreams work— that I have driven onto the top of the drugstore soda fountain counter like the one where my father and I used to eat coddies and drink chocolate sodas on Dolfield Road in Baltimore while my mother got her hair done next door. He liked the chocolate soda better than I did. I always wanted an ice cream soda and he could be counted on to get me one.

I am lost but dream: D. waits with his arms open. He kisses me full on the mouth, deeply, with desire, and with admiration if one can feel that in a kiss. I think one can.

He is so slim, so beautiful and in real life so totally unattainable.

I send him a poem by Auden with the note: Remember this? Here is a brief excerpt:

> *Lullaby*
>
> *Lay your sleeping head, my love,*
>
> *Human on my faithless arm;*
>
> *. . .*
>
> *Not a whisper, not a thought,*
>
> *Not a kiss nor look be lost. . . .*

Remember? I ask.

M.

And he replies:

> Think not lost, perhaps nearly born.
>
> D.

I recall D.'s heart and being like the drift of the Caribbean sea over the sand, the strand of light that reaches through the clarity of that sea. His touch and his kiss that once expressed *his* clarity that took me in its sight and held me so that I let go, floated in its buoyant assurance.

I may not know what I am doing but I do know that what I have just written bears itself on the incontrovertible.

I must understand the multiplicity of irreducible people, of the irreducible D., and that my humanity lies therein. We will not have perfection in discourse. But I must seek humanity in discourse. That responsibility weighs heavily on me as I think it should.

And so, I wave. I wait for the sea.

One Game at a Time

D. makes me think about baseball. In particular about Albert Pujols.

> Pujols . . . really does take 'em one game at a time, one at-bat at a time, one pitch at a time . . . Questions are beside the point. Talk is beside the point. The point for Albert Pujols is to hit the ball hard. Everything else is just noise," Joe Posnanski wrote in *Sports Illustrated*.
>
> This doesn't make him especially fun to approach after a game, even a two-home run game. But it's part of what makes him the best baseball player on earth. And it's what makes him likely to have many more two-homer games, even if he isn't a home run hitter.

With D.: no answers to questions. Silence.

D. makes me think, too, of the movie *Juno*: *Juno* is a sweet flick about a sixteen-year-old who makes love *once* with her boyfriend, her initiation into sex with only the motive of love, and she gets pregnant. She decides to have the baby and give it away to a couple that really wants a baby. She says she's ill-equipped to raise a baby. She is a wise, sharp-tongued, witty and oddly sweet character. Sweet in her sharpness. And at the end, when she's had the baby, her boyfriend comes to the hospital in his running clothes and gets in the bed and lies down and holds her.

My heart broke at this image, because this is the way D. used to lie down at night with me. We didn't make love—no home run to continue the metaphor—

but we did lie down together, body on body.

I became angry with D. *again* the night I watched the movie on DVD with him.

D. had been anything but a "husband." He hadn't made love to me willingly anyway in so many years I could calculate the time in terms of a decade, a wall of time, a block so large that it stood in the way of vision, my recollection of the past. I have talked about this too much here. I now know I am a fool for having done so. Fools repeat their mistakes—except in Shakespeare's plays where the fool speaks wisdom: In *Lear*, the fool wisely says:

> He that has and a tiny little wit—
> With hey, ho, the wind and the rain—
> Must make content with his fortunes fit,
> For the rain it raineth every day.

But that night, I was thinking about the fact of lack of sex as the source of all my trouble, fool without wisdom that I was. After the movie, I drank myself through our take-out-Chinese dinner—I live a block from Chinatown. I drank my way through D.'s silence.

What was he to do with my anger?

I recalled for him how hard *alone* has been. I recanted nights with my chest full of anxiety that raged so hard I couldn't eat, mornings with my head hung over. Nights I didn't have the energy to shower. Nights when my teaching work was done and still I couldn't eat. I recounted all those nights I worked on the separation agreement *again*. The nights I had a vodka and tonic. How that made the anxiety subside, how when hunger appeared, I ate a frozen pizza and cooked some asparagus. I recalled how my kitchen and my body were low on food because I don't have a car—and getting food via metro in D.C. is not at all the way I thought it would be when I moved here, when I thought a small grocer, Balducci's, was gonna be here. Expensive but close. They backed out of that deal while I was in Missouri.

I recanted the night I had finally gotten the pot rack hung in my apartment, the same pot rack I'd had in our house. How I'd finally gotten all the copper and stainless steel pots hung. I'd polished the copper. Even though I did not have the energy to cook, I was ready to cook—but did not cook.

D. listened. He was silent but he listened. You gotta admire his restraint. And then he went home.

And then I slept but woke at 2 a.m. from a terror: My kitchen. In the dream my son came to visit—my son who has not spoken to D. since D. left me. He swiftly took down all the pots. The pot rack wasn't there. Just some hooks in the ceiling. He had cleaned up what he viewed as my mess. I called out: Where are they, where are my pots and pans? Where is my bain marie, my French copper and enamel double boiler that I used to melt chocolate, that I scrambled eggs in, that I loved. I find instead dolls and children's clown costumes. I'd made these costumes for my daughter and son when they were little. I'd made one for myself too. I'd made one for D. after my first husband had betrayed me. But in the dream the only costume I can find is the one I'd made for myself—the pink gingham one.

For the fool does need the costume.

When I am awake, this costume is the only one that *is* lost. I have all the others in a box in a closet that D. built for me this year—*after* the separation agreement was finally done. After it was clear that we would live apart, that we are *done*.

After all that, he gave me money to build out the closets in my 1200 square foot loft with virtually no storage. The loft where I am making a life—alone: *where I make content with my fortunes fit.*

He did this after he'd come over to drop off miss-delivered mail—an excuse? He could have forwarded the mail. He gave me money for the closets after he found me throwing out the clown costumes, the sweaters my mother had made for my children, the dress she'd made for me in 6th grade, after he found me in tears, throwing away what I could not store.

Now all is stored away in my California-Closet-re-done apartment where I live alone.

And then he sent an e-mail. The subject line was: "I know this is against the rules but— Would you like to go to the Nationals baseball game Thursday night? They're playing the Cardinals. Really good seats. Red, Hot and Blue barbeque. Or Ben's Chili Bowl."

I didn't go to the game where I would have seen Albert Pujols at bat.

I said I couldn't go because we were *done*, because I needed to move *on*, because I couldn't bear the *silence*.

And then he spoke. He wrote:

M.,

I do love you and always have. I have in the past only known how to show love through care-taking. I never learned any other way. But that is no longer enough. I know I need to show it in other ways, most especially through emotional intimacy. I can tell you I love you, but it sounds hollow because there is, right now, no other action behind it. I know that is how it appears, so it is hard for me to say it to you. I just know my feelings are deep, and it is not just history, important as that is. I have always thought and said that I believe we will end up together. I still believe that. But I know it is very hard for you. I don't want to lose you, but I also don't want to hurt you again. That is how I am torn. It is hard; it is painful. I hope and pray that it will work out. I just want you to know that I do love you and care deeply for you.

D.

All this makes me think of Albert Pujols. He avoids reporters. When he does talk to them, he doesn't answer their questions. He just keeps going to bat.

All this makes me think of the movie *Juno*: When all goes wrong, how to set things right?

And I answer: One at-bat at a time.

Once D. asked me, What do you call a player who strikes out two out of three times?

He answered: A hall of famer.

Light

When a photographer uses a filter, a transparent or translucent disc, on his lens, he alters the light. If a flock of geese appeared on a clear day—cumulus clouds, horizontal white streaks on blue—and the photographer placed a lens on his camera's eye, for a black and white photo—as if that term, black-and-white, accurately defines a photo without color—the lens turns the clouds gray as on a dark day, and the bird's wings white, their undersides, shadows of their shapes.

How we see: Through a scrim.

On August 25 my parent's anniversary, I wrote when I began to tell—like a child "telling"—and so I repeat here, childishly repeat: They were married fifty-four years. Can you believe it?

"I need to live alone," he said. Oh so Greta Garbo.

There was absolutely no noise.

But how to see my way? That is the question. Is that not always the question?

Bird on a wire, out of the cage.

Nietzsche says, *He who would learn to fly one day must first learn to stand and walk and run and climb and dance; one cannot fly into flying.*

When D. and I went to see *The Reader*, the movie, based on the book, about the woman who teaches herself to read—first I touched his arm to reach for it. He said, "Don't pull on my sleeve." In the movie, he bought popcorn.

We are on a date. I am moved by him despite the gesture of dismissal, moved by all that I've known of him.

This is the man who left me.

I eat a handful of popcorn, reach to touch his head, the head he shaves—smooth like a baby's bottom. My thirty-five-year-old daughter has had a child. D. thinks of my daughter as *his* daughter. A birth, a new life in a new marriage.

Again he pushes me away. "Greasy," he says, as if that mattered, as if I'd muss his hair, as if the popcorn were buttered. It is not.

I recall: After we'd sold the house, after I'd taken the job as a visiting writer at U. of Missouri, he invited me to a wine tasting at the Greek Embassy—this man who did not want me though he'd not said that. After that awful Greek Embassy thing (barely any food that you had to fight for and zillions of people standing in line for wine), he wanted to take me out some place; I wanted to go home, but we went to Cloud in Dupont Circle. I asserted, "You don't desire me. Tell me." "No," he said.

Like the O ring on the Challenger that exploded in the sky—from where we stood watching through a lens: no noise. Like the O ring when placed in 32-degree water. "The O ring, a large key to the problem," the investigator said. Indeed, it would not give, it wouldn't expand or contract—frozen.

We were frozen.

After *The Reader*, when we get to my condo . . . Gone: the house with the chef's kitchen, the four-story one-hundred-year-old Victorian we'd renovated like a wish fulfilled . . . D. stays with me. We watch *The Thomas Crown Affair*, the second version, the one with Pierce Brosnan, the financier and art thief who takes a hundred-thousand-dollar bet on a golf swing from a sand-trap the day after he'd stolen the Monet, and Rene Russo, the insurance investigator who wants to nail him, get his head—you know that he loves her: When he gives her the controls on his glider that slides through the sky with no motor— "Like a hawk"—when he brushes his hand across her hair. While they are window shopping, when he stands behind her, his head down, when he takes hold of her shoulders, the slight brush of his hands.

No noise.

I wake in the middle of the night, know that he must go, that I am returning to territory I know too well: backtracking.

I backtrack: a dream: My father lies in a bed, my dead mother stands near. An official-looking man, clipboard in hand, asks him questions. He says to me, "I know you hate me." I say, "I don't hate you because I believe you know that my father's intelligence and wry sense of humor drive his answers." The clipboard-man persists, says that my father's answer to his last question confirms that he cannot live on his own: assisted living needed, nursing home more likely. "So what was the question?" I ask. "If you are outside, on open grass and see an object coming toward you, what do you do?" "And his answer?" I ask. "Golf."

In the morning, we make love and, as we begin, I say, "The trouble with you is," and he says, "Only one trouble?" I say, "The trouble with you is that I love you." And he says, "That's not the trouble. That makes all things possible."

I look out a window. Sky and water merge and in the mix I see iridescent blue-black birds, yellow-blue-black fish on limbs of trees. Through the glass, safe inside a house with a large kitchen, my pots hang again. But how could fish and fowl, light and small as they are come to my tree? How could they, so rare in size and startled color, come so close to me?

The answer is, *Whoever would become light and a bird . . .*

Photo by Andy Duback (www.andyduback.com)

33

Forget Paris

I read in *The Washington Post* a movie review of *Paris*. Ann Hornaday says, "Cédric Klapisch's intoxicating portrait of a city that, despite (or more likely, *because of*) being in a state of constant flux, retains timeless energy and allure."

I have not seen the movie that is playing at E Street but I plan to go instead of going to Paris. It is hard to go to the city of love without love. I had been thinking of Paris because my daughter and son-in-law and granddaughter, hurtling onto five months and wowing the Parisians, are there.

Paris equals love: the too-oft used equation of the romantic comedy.

Hornaday to my surprise does not mention that Cédric Klapisch has directed two of my all-time favorite movies that I classify as Parisian romantic comedies—an off-classification that suits me perfectly because the Rom-Com that fits that term too well has usually lost its edge. These have not: *L'Auberge Espagnole* (filmed in Spain) and *Russian Dolls* (Paris, London, St. Petersburg) are edgy.

Meanwhile, as in yesterday, the CEO I'd met on the plane home from Australia—my Ezio Pinza (*across a crowded room . . .*)—wrote me again. This time to say that his "love" has died. "My love" is the way he has always referred to the woman he was on his way to see when he met me on the plane from San Francisco to D.C., the woman he'd been dating since he met her on a high-end cruise—meaning not many people, small boat—after his wife had died.

Last we talked on the phone ever so briefly I told him things with D. were in flux and in play.

He writes, "I probably should not be sending this since our connection lapsed so long ago." He explains what has happened and ends with, "It is as I said at the beginning, 'I probably should not . . . his ellipsis].' Yet at times like this, perhaps we need to cut ourselves a bit of slack."

I sit in front of the e-mail: I ponder him. I ponder me. I ponder D. I reply with words about mourning, with my own realization that, as I say to him, "I can only imagine how this loss has thrown you back into the déjà vu of your beloved wife. As to my husband [or rather D. as we know him here] I say that the story of our relationship "is an open book for all to read. I am writing a blog, have been doing so for a year now."

I wonder now about the CEO: A missed chance that was probably not a chance that the CEO never allowed to *be* in his honorable stance and his privacy? I gather that he has kept quite a distance from his east coast "love" as he lives comfortably with cook and housekeeper in Saratoga and retreats often to his house in Carmel—no phone, no computer—to paint and collect, perhaps for a book, the letters of his wife.

I wonder D.—as in, I *worry* him. His presence pervades this writing and, I now see, all the preceding chapters here. You don't need to say it. I will: *She's not moved on.*

As synchronicity would have it, as I was reaching for Joan Didion's *The Year of Magical Thinking* and for T.S. Eliot's *Selected Poems* because I sought something to quote to the CEO from these works, a small torn-edged card falls out of one of the books: the note from the brief encounter in the galley on the plane: his e-mail address and this line in his hand, "Cooking is an over-rated feminine attribute," a reference to the title of my first book, the title that appeared in the margin of the blog, much as it appeared in the margin of my life (instead of celebration, separation).

I write to the CEO that virtually everyone describes grief as coming in waves—sudden and overwhelming.

I say that the death of a parent or a sibling, as I have lost both my parents and my sister, is like a break in the sea. Now I read this and see that my description of grief likens, oddly to love.

The miracle of Didion's book is that she never once mentions the word *love* while she writes a love story. In her book, she describes the dailiness of her life with her husband; she has her own list.

I have mine: espresso and steamed milk in the morning. Cuban bread made quickly with three packages of dried yeast, the baked bread devoured with lightening speed what has lightened with time. Pea soup from Craig Claiborne's *New York Times Cookbook*. Beef stewed in red wine and tomatoes, string beans added at the end. Fork-stirred omelets rolled onto his plate.

Didion quotes from Eliot's "The Wasteland" with no reference; in others words, you either know the source or not: "These fragments I have shored against my ruins." p. 190-1 in her book. This is line 431 in "The Wasteland," in part V *What the Thunder Said*, three lines from the poem's end.

The CEO ends his e-mail this way, "Incidentally, I've reread two poems you sent to me, 'Leap Before You Look' and 'The Privilege of Being,' . . . [his ellipsis] both compelling."

The first is an all time favorite of mine by Auden; the second, a poem by Robert Hass that has resonated throughout my life.

I now ponder whether either of these poems would fill up the ellipsis of time that has passed between me and this gorgeous seventy-ish, stylish, loyal, sensitive man.

I reread. The poems, as poetry magically does, answer:

In "Leap Before You Look," Auden says, *The sense of danger must not disappear*, that we must not consent to *never mention those who disappear* and that *although I love you, you will have to leap; /Our dream of safety has to disappear.*

I like to think I have lived by these words, but knowing oneself is the work of a lifetime. So, who knows? But whether I have lived the words or not, they ring like bells. They answer.

Hass's poem answers with stunning reality and Victorian swoon—Wisdom more often than not comprises paradox. In "Privilege of Being," Hass talks of the angels up above *in the unshaken ether and crystal of human longing* as they watch those making love in that awkward pose of ecstasy and he reminds *that life has limits, that people die young, fail at love, /fail of their ambitions.*

But love is the human wish.

I think, Maybe Paris? More soon . . . (ellipsis mine).

Hat trick

After seeing the movie *Paris* with D., we go to sit on his balcony and drink good red wine that I cannot name though I would like to say it was French, suspect it was Spanish—we are a little drunk. His apartment is near the Verizon Center and the Capitals are playing. We are so close that we can hear the blare of horns. When he checks the scores, we learn that the Caps are beating Toronto three-zip. D. thinks that Alexander Ovechkin may have a "hat trick": three goals in one game. But it turns out that Ovechkin has two goals and one assist. Not bad. Final score Caps 6, Maple Leafs 4. I read the next day *Washington AP*: "By the time the game was 77 seconds old, Alex Ovechkin scored the first time his stick touched the puck, earning 'MVP!' chants from all those red-clad fans." Surely he will get the hat trick again the way he did in May 2009 against the Pittsburgh Penguins.

I am stuck on the hat trick. For me the movie *Paris* is Cédric Klapisch's and his favorite male lead Romain Duris's hat trick: *L'Auberge Espagnole* (filmed in Spain) and *Russian Dolls* (Paris, London, St. Petersburg) and now a window on Paris from a non-Rom-Com view that includes Romain Duris's view of the city from a taxi. In that one scene we see Rom-Com Paris: the Tour Eiffel, the golden statue, a Rom-Com collage but not as I have ever seen anything in that much-filmed city filmed—not as I perceive the city by then. For Klapisch has closed with the hat trick.

What we have seen by then is the refrigerated fruit and vegetable outlet while in most Parisian movies we see romanced markets in the street. We see them here too but with the gloss from the grit of living. We see refrigerated meat lockers. We see flowers pushed on an industrial cart by a strong young working-class woman. We see academic Paris. We see dancing, dream-like Paris (Romain Duris, slim beauty in red) and tiny apartments that bespeak living in the spaces of the heart—not the spaces of *Architectural Digest*.

No villains and no heroes. Humanity on full compassionate show culminating in the simple exchange that brought me to full tears: "Merci" and "merci aussi," built on the relationship of the characters played by Romain Duris and Juliette Binoche who speak these words.

When we leave the theater, D. asks me, as he makes a note to himself in his Blackberry, "It was Bach's Minuet in G Major?" And I am struck that he hears what I do not hear, that he brings music to me. He seduced me with his piano, the one with the crack in its sounding board, the one he sold when he married me. He had little furniture when I met him, had placed his baby grand as the centerpiece of his living area.

In 1984 he called me and told me he had a gift for me and I should come over from my place, a tiny house in Garrett Park estates—meaning that all the old big Victorians were in Garrett Park and that I lived in the estate, the extensive land where the poor live near the rich. We used to call his apartment up on Pooks Hill *California* because the kids and I went there to swim in his pool, to sit on his balcony, to stand in the shiny-like-marble glistening lobby—a world apart. I came that day and he played Beethoven's "Pathétique" and then without words, with instead the simple silence that follows the end of a piece, the laying of his hands in his lap, he looked at me. And I wept. I'd wept from the first melodic chord.

This was the last time he played the piano for me—twenty-eight years ago. When we lived together, I often heard him work on Schubert's Impromptu in G Flat but he's never played it for me all the way through. The barren period. Music in silence. When I heard him play, I'd be upstairs in our large Victorian house in Adams Morgan—we'd come such a long way but not come through.

All the silence would seem to me to be gone when I heard him play.

A piano teacher once told me the story about the man who was lucky enough the night before a concert to get a hotel room next to Rubenstein, or was it Horowitz? She'd forgotten which, the name did not matter. What mattered was that the man heard through the wall the same phrase played over and over and over, like a needle stuck on a scratch in a record.

D. and I are stuck like that.

Before all the loss, when I watched him play that day he seduced me, I saw the muscles in his shoulders, his forearms, the angle of his back. The movement of his brow, the corner of his mouth, the line beside his eye. I watched his body move through the piece. He leaned into the bass. The melody rang from the keys, shifted in tone, in softness and loudness with his touch. His back curved into the music, his brow softened, his shoulders rose and fell with the thematic repetition. His neck bent and relaxed.

What he does not know is that when I heard the Schubert in G as I lay in the bed where I waited for him, where I often fell asleep before he came to bed, I did not hear the missed notes, the imperfect phrasing that he explained as the reasons he could not play for me or anyone else. I thought I heard his heart pulse, but knew it was my own.

I am stuck on the hat trick: Will he pull Bach's Minuet in G Major out of his? Will I pull Paris out of mine?

When Alex Ovechkin pulls the trick, the ice will be full of hats. This tradition owes its history to cricket when a bowler knocked off three wickets and was awarded with a hat.

I am reminded of my favorite Rom-Com *The Thomas Crown Affair*—not the first one with Steve McQueen and Faye Dunaway, but the second with Pierce Brosnan and Rene Russo. Tommy hides by wearing a bowler hat and filling the museum with men in bowler hats, an allusion to the painting "Son of Man" by René Magritte: a man who wears a suit and a bowler hat with an apple on his face.

When we truly see, we see what has been hidden: the hat trick.

Bedtrick

Last week I reminded D. about Canada and he answered, Clive Owen. One of Owen's movies we both love is entitled *Duplicity*. No one is who they seem to be.

When we were together we often spoke in code to one another. For days on end we couldn't remember the name of the actress in Hitchcock's *North by Northwest*, a movie we both love because no one is who they seem. We'd come up with Lee Remick when it was Eva Marie Saint. From then on whenever either one of us couldn't remember something, the other would say "Lee Remick," as code for the problem and the movie we both loved—and we'd laugh.

Neither of us is who we seem: separated and free to choose. Learning this has been a journey that seems a bit like *The Wizard of Oz*, the movie most of us grew up with where Dorothy wears ruby slippers, magical shoes that she does not learn until story's end will send her home with a click of her heels.

We were two years separated when D. asked me to go to Canada with him: French Canada: Montreal, Quebec. We entered the elegant Hotel Nelligan on the old street near the water, 106 Saint-Paul West. French spoken everywhere.

We ate soft boiled eggs in the morning, croissants we tried unsuccessfully to resist. We drank good French wine, ate good bistro steak salads or Asian salmon in the evenings, sitting on their upper deck trying to remember Clive Owen's name.

We slept in a double-sheeted bed on 400-thread-count linens. In the best hotels, your blanket lies inside a duvet with another flat sheet on top so that all you feel are the crisp clean sheets each night you climb into bed.

But I felt short-sheeted on this trip. Remember that prank? Short-sheeted because I waited for D. to make love to me: We were on vacation together. We were sleeping in the same bed. On day five of the trip, I asked, "Will we make love?" He answered, "I would like to."

This makes me think of Wendy Doniger's book *The Bedtrick*, where she begins this way,

> You go to bed with someone you know, and when you wake up you discover that it was someone else—another man or another woman, or a woman instead of a man, or a god, or a snake or a foreigner or alien, or a complete stranger or your own wife or husband, or your mother or father. This is what Shakespearean scholars call 'the bedtrick'—sex with a partner who pretends to be someone else.

In her prologue she refers us to plays we know where not knowing who is who intrigues and answers: In Edmond Rostand's *Cyrano de Bergerac* and the film version *Roxanne*, a movie with Steve Martin and Darryl Hannah that I love. In Shakespeare's *Twelfth Night*, a play I often return to for Feste the jester's words when accused by Maria, Olivia's lady-in-waiting: *My lady will hang thee for thy absence*, and Feste answers, *Let her hang me. He that is well-hanged in this world needs to fear no colors,* with its proverbial dare and its double entendre and where the fool is anything but.

Let me embarrass D. further by telling you that he is indeed well-hung— thus, my despair in Canada.

We were a long way from Paris, my metaphor for the Rom-Com ending.

Let us now use Canada as the metaphor for marriage.

When we return, I assume that we are reconciling. But he tells me all must remain the same. He is not ready. I am inconsolable. I seek counseling. I seek an exit strategy: Emergency egress. Do not retract dead bolt.

I write him. It is a last ditch effort that speaks for its desperate self. Trust me: What follows does not speak well for me:

Dear D.,

I miss you. I've been missing you for a long time I now realize.

I know I am angry but I am still very much in love with you. You have hurt me so deeply that I fear I may never recover, may never be able to love another and may never be able to fully part from you. I sometimes think I am going to die from this heartbreak and what I perceive as your coolness towards me. You have been cool towards me for so long that I don't think you even know how long. But I have waited. I was waiting. I am still waiting. I am quite mixed up and what I write will probably anger you. I fear that anger so profoundly that I hardly know where to start. But I cannot help the fact that I still must admit that I love you even if I can never have with you what I thought we once had and maybe did have.

I need to be loved again, desired again, fought for, if you will. I know that is too much to ask.

I am offering my hand to you. I know that I offer that hand with much trepidation and that I want some things to be made up to me, childish as that is.

I can no longer cry my way back to you. I have done too much of that over the years and have been deeply wounded by weeping in closets and on floors and in desperation to get you back. I can no longer have you that way. I don't want anyone that way; I don't ever again want to be humiliated the way I have been. But I still believe that we may have something that we built and that is worth saving. But I cannot keep trying to get you alone. I must know that you are trying to get me, too.

Eventually, I may wear out and move on, whether or not I can find love. I may move on out of loneliness. I may have to as I crave intimacy so, don't really find life worth living without it. I don't mean that as a threat. I mean it as E.M. Forster says in his epigraph to *Howard's End*: 'Only connect . . .' He defines who I am in the world and who I must be. But you are inside me, and that will never change.

We will live apart. We must now. I finally understand that. But what I have written is worth saying, I think.

Mary

His reply: Of course I've saved it, for here is the bedtrick*:

M,

My reaction to this is anything but anger. I don't react angrily to much anymore. On the contrary, what you write is so heartfelt, it is deeply touching. I know I have been cool, but it doesn't mean I don't have similar feelings for you. I could not have gotten so deep inside you without you getting just as deep inside me. My coolness is, I guess ironically, part of my healing, at least initially. I know you are frustrated by this and want to be 'engaged' and part of my healing. But I am afraid—afraid of doing the same things to you that I did before.

The potential for damage and setbacks is still great. I need get to some level of confidence about myself. I don't know that I can explain better at this point, but I hope you can somehow accept that, for now. I do want to be engaged with you, but it may be less intimate right now than you would prefer. Please know that I am aware of that—I am beginning to understand what intimacy is. And while it is not yet what you want, please also know that I am trying to get there.

D.

I have come to understand that what I think I know, I don't know.

Case in point: Did you know that Dorothy's shoes in L. Frank Baum's book were silver?**

We had been to Canada. Where is Paris? It is not on any map. That is the bedtrick.

To find Paris, ask this question: Who needs ruby slippers?

---

*When I told D. I wanted couples therapy not to get back together, but for an exit strategy, he said, "I don't want an exit." He sought his own therapist. We were then both with separate psychiatrists: Were we in a Woody Allen film? All together now, let us click our heels.

**You can follow the yellow brick road or listen to Nietzsche who says, *He who would learn to fly one day must first learn to stand and walk and run and climb and dance; one cannot fly into flying.*

Run and See

I am stuck on romantic comedies: good ones, middling ones, the watch-me-over-and-over again ones: *Runaway Bride* is like a children's book for me. Remember when you were a kid and your mother or father read you a story before you went to bed and you said, "Read it again"? It's that way for me with *Runaway Bride*.

It was that way for me with *The Runaway Bunny*, the Margaret Wise Brown classic—but not as you'd expect: Yes, my children loved the book but I actually don't remember it from my own childhood. I recall it from reading it to them, to Ben and to Sarah, and wanting to read it again and again—more now than when my children were small and needed to be read to, needed to be tucked in.

I have watched *Runaway Bride* more times than I would like to admit—as if its formula will serve up the answer to my dilemma, the dilemma of the woman who's been dumped—or so she thought. It's not as if the evidence wasn't real: D. *did* leave, the house *is* sold. But these are the trappings of loss. Something at the center of this seeming disaster awaits discovery.

So, I turn to *Runaway Bride*: The bride who runs away in the Garry Marshall film is played by Julia Roberts. This bride runs at successive weddings. She runs like the runaway bunny to find herself and still be safe. Julia's character runs from the hippie rock singer, the broken-hearted-soon-to-be priest, the entomologist, the football coach and even from Richard Gere, playing a journalist-wanna-be novelist, who does truly get her, who knows that she ate her eggs the same way every man she's been engaged to ate his. It's a tired metaphor that in the Rom-Com works as we watch her lay out the eggs prepared as she once ate them in each former relationship: scrambled, poached, fried, egg-whites-only omelet—and finally Benedict—not Arnold—her final choice when she is ready to give up her running shoes and wed.

Benedict Arnold—the general who changed sides during the Revolutionary War, who joined the British when the colonies were seeking their freedom—has nothing to do with Julia's egg choice and everything to do with why we run away: The treason for which his name has become synonymous is inextricably tied to the struggle to be independent. I could argue that I was betrayed but perhaps identity was at stake: both D.'s and mine.

I am no longer sure of who needed more to run: D. or me.

I often dream of D. and the sea: At the beach. I want so to go to the beach. But a man has come to my house by the sea to say that someone is going to be killed. Someone is watching the house in a car. I must lie down below the windows so that I'm not seen. I have asked that D. come across the beach to meet me, but I cannot go out. I'm afraid to go out. He is on the beach and though it is warm out he is wearing his cashmere watch cap and his coat. The water is sliding up on the beach, clear and blue and covered with foam. I don't go out at first because I know that someone is going to be killed. But there D. stands alone, waiting. I go onto the beach but he is gone. Another man tries to give me a package. I won't take the small package because I know what is inside: Something wrapped in sausage skin, like a disembodied penis. I refuse. I walk on the sand, put my feet in the water.

I wake thinking it is morning. But it is only 2 a.m. and I am tired. I think it is morning because the street lights, or is it the moon? cast a glow inside my bedroom.

Like most dreams this one makes no sense and total sense. Its Freudian implications seem clear: disembodied penis and all. But I am drawn to the light cast by the moon with the love of the sea in my heart. I lie alone in bed only to discover that the someone who is going to be killed is me.

Like the runaway bride, I must choose my own eggs: I must kill the self that could not be seen.

My daughter had a boyfriend who gave her *The Runaway Bunny* after they had parted: I recall this suitor as a smothering blanket. Run, Run, I thought, when she finally ended the affair. His gift copy of the book sits inappropriately on *my* bookshelf with his inscription (not mine to reveal) on the facing page. His contact info below his words lies like an unfulfilled wish. My daughter Sarah, self in tact, is married now and in Paris—the one that's on the map.

In the Rom-Com, Paris is *not* on any map.

And I am soon to runaway there: the trip is planned. Which will it be? Paris on the map or Paris in the Rom-Com?

As we now know I am obsessed with Rom-Coms because in the good ones wisdom and fantasy meet. Watch *Runaway Bride* and wait for the speech that Richard Gere's character states and that Julia's later repeats. It goes like this: *I guarantee that we will have tough times. I guarantee that at some point one or both of us will want to get out. But I also guarantee that if I don't ask you to be mine, I'll regret it for the rest of my life.*

I am in the tough times and the gettin' out time. What to do?

Watch another Rom-Com.

In *The Thomas Crown Affair* that I also watch over and over again, the painting by René Magritte *Son of Man* plays a key role as its image of a man who wears a suit and a bowler hat with an apple on his face appears again and again. Tommy, played by Pierce Brosnan, is that enigmatic man who will soon be known: life as he knew it erased but self fully in tact.

In a book I love by John Berger entitled *About Looking,* Berger quotes Magritte on his view of paintings as "material signs of the freedom of thought . . . Life, the Universe, the Void, have no value for thought when it is truly free. The only thing that has value for it is Meaning that is the moral concept of the Impossible." Berger comments, "To conceive of the impossible is difficult. Magritte knew this." And later in the essay Berger adds, "If a painting by Magritte confirms one's lived experience to date, it has by his standards, failed; if it temporarily destroys that experience, it has succeeded. (This destruction is the only fearful thing in his art.)"

I have feared the destruction of my perceived experience, of my illusory self. But I now know that in destruction lies discovery.

So, I will run to Paris, but I will run with this knowledge: That I am both the runaway bunny and the runaway bride.

Let the Rom-Com roll, for my role in it emerges the way the apple in Magritte's painting cancels out the face, and in its absence, holds before me the chance to *see*.

Transom

I am about to travel to Paris. And before I embark, I contemplate the journey at stake.

In Kate Chopin's *The Awakening*, published in 1899, Chopin's main character says,

> I would give up the unessential; I would give my money. I would give my life for my children; but I wouldn't give myself, I can't make it any clearer; it's only something which I am beginning to comprehend, which is revealing itself to me.

Like the character in Chopin's novel, I am on the journey of discovering the totality of self—if that is ever possible.

Though writers (beware of the critic) and people who hope and fantasize are cautioned to be careful of dreams, I look to my dreams for answers about who I am. Here's one: Keys on a thin metal ring. Collecting the keys of others, of boys so that they may not leave class, go back to their apartments. Beethoven playing. We in class are studying him section by section. The students are both kids and young men. My father's face at the transom.

I must want D.'s keys. I must want him playing Beethoven. Or do I?

The old Victorian in Adams Morgan where D. and I lived had old doors with transoms and mullioned windows that one doesn't see in condos in downtown D.C. I miss the house on Kalorama Road, my library, my writing room.

Or do I?

The houses have all gone under the sea.

At the gym some time ago, a beautiful married woman who wears diamonds to work out, asked me how I was. I said, "Lots of dates but no one." "Would a man really make you happy?" she asked. I answered, "I think so." But I wonder. Isn't this a good question for me? Perhaps I have found my place in the world.

After all Thoreau went off to the woods and we are still reading him. What was his loneliness about? Or what was his solitude about, a better question.

And here I sit, ready to fly, with the longing for emotional memory, for the holding of life.

Last night I was watching Julian Schnabel's *The Diving Bell and the Butterfly*. If that man with locked-in syndrome could do what he did, can I not do this? I can, I can.

I want to be the little engine that could. I want to recall those moments with Sarah, my philosopher daughter with her first book coming out in May, and with Ben, my son who is so hard on me now—he has no use for D.

I long for our moments on the couch in the family room, watching Mr. Rogers. *I like you just the way you are.* What a comfort I found Mr. Rogers to be. I recall the yellow Dansk pot that I made Sarah's "chocky" (her hot chocolate) in. The pouring of the hot liquid into her cup, her little hands pounding on the table, announcing her impatience. I recall Ben when he was ten or eleven, standing in a doorway watching me cook. My children are grown now. One is in Paris where I will go; the other, in Australia on his vineyard.

I feel as if I am at the transom, high above the door frame looking through frosted glass at the life that lies before me, or better, at the one I am living, watching the way my father watched from the transom of my classroom in my dream. I feel him with me in the way I used to feel my mother after she died. He has been dead nine years and I feel him in the way I felt her then, as if he is coming to me.

I sense that my sexuality is involved here for my father was key to its emergence, to my sense of what it is like to be loved by a man. Did his fears infiltrate that knowing? I have described my father's quiet, his calm like the sense of the sea receding with the tide; his angles like a Giacometti sculpture in shadow at the edge of sand in fading light. But the flip side of his quiet was an abiding fear that he would lose one of us.

When he was old, some months after my mother had died, I was moved by the angles of his body at the edge of the sea. He stood on a beach in Hilton Head. D. and I had taken him with us on a business/vacation trip where we could swim, play tennis (my father used a Western grip and had a slice that could place the ball at the corner of the court). That day at the beach, D. went out far in the ocean to swim. My father walked the edge of the shore until D. came in, some forty minutes later. He must have watched me and my sister, both good swimmers, in that same way.

He came to his fears through loss: His mother and father came through a sewer with my father's oldest sibling, an infant at my grandmother's breast, during a pogrom in Russia when they left their parents and the life they knew to emerge on the other end in freedom. Much was gained, but the loss does not fade. I carry that loss and more because all my grandparents died before I was born and because I have lived through the devastating illnesses and deaths of my mother, my sister and my father. I wonder if my fear of loss is a legacy that I carry with me like the memory of my father and the way he paced the shore.

As I free myself or rather try to free myself from those fears, I sense my father's face at the transom of my life. I hear his wish: *It is time for you to do what I could not.*

A transom is a strengthening cross bar set above a window or a door. I am looking for a crossbar that gives me strength. A mullion is the vertical bar between the panes of glass. Do mullions and transoms form the pattern of a window, a window on what is next?

I see a woman at a house by the sea, a loose white dress, and the breeze across her face. I see a grassy plot where tea and wine and wind will begin the story.

My Apartment!

I am finally in Paris and can't believe it: 125 square feet, small French appliances with minds of their own, window on the courtyard: all at 7 Rue des Francs Bourgeois. Peace and quiet surrounded by the hubbub of Paris, beautiful stores with treasures I ogle. Want to write in my little attic room but Paris, irresistible.

Chapter

39

French Subtitles

Have you ever seen an American movie with French subtitles? Jim Jarmusch had a new film *Limits of Control* that I went to see while in Paris. Here is the preview link:

http://www.mk2.com/filmscinema-5257-thelimitsofcontrol.html

Click on the tiny camera icon to view the trailer.

Before I went, I wondered if seeing a movie in the language I speak with subtitles in the language of the country where I am would be like discovering the unconscious? I am full of questions in Paris and discovery awaits me. This I know of all the things I do not know.

This and the fact that the city of lights is also the city of parks. I want to live here.

Doors

Limits of Control, Jim Jarmusch's film about art and life and what we can and cannot control, perhaps about how we know what we think we know ran at the theater next to the Bibliothèque Nationale de France, the glass towers of books that go on and on and on—that Sebold writes about in *Austerlitz*—and that you cannot enter unless you know the code: how I think about the doors, the maze one must follow to find the doors. Actually, you can buy a reader's card, but you cannot go into the stacks, the towers that dominate the horizon on the edge of old Paris. The reading room seduces the way my solitude does. Does my solitude reveal?

    I plan to go to the Pompidou: One exhibit: THE SUBVERSION OF IMAGES, SURREALISM, PHOTOGRAPHY, FILM—but the staff is on strike. How

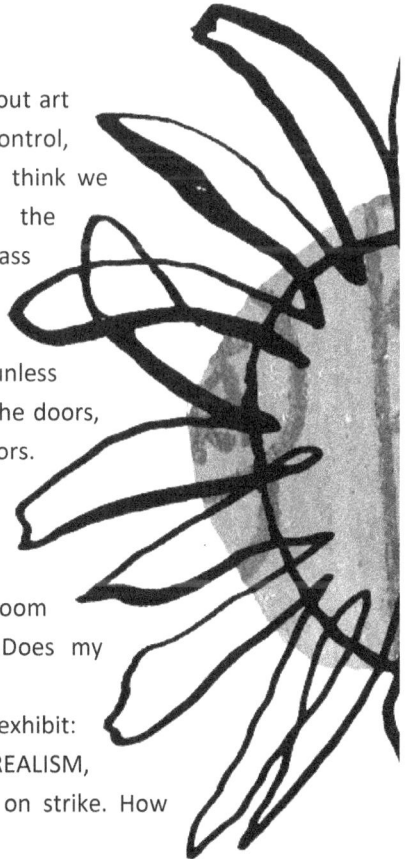

appropriate: unable to get in to see the surreal. I stand outside and look the way I stood outside the library.

I think, What is the code? Send in the clowns, the fools, the genies and whoever else can help.

Bridges

The days are short in Paris: sunrise in winter at 8:38, sunset at 4:53: Check your city and compare at Sunrise Sunset. (http://www.sunrisesunset.com/)

After the long walk west on Rue des Francs-Bourgeois that turns into Rue Rambuteau to the closed Pompidou, I returned to stand by the Seine at Quai Henry IV near my apartment as the sun took its slide down. Take a look at:

http://www.abcgallery.com/R/rousseau/rousseau46.html

I have heard that it is easy to be without love in Paris. But as the bateau slides with the setting sun, I can think only of Audrey Hepburn and Cary Grant when she kisses him and, if I remember correctly, she says, "Can't kiss back?" And then he does. And again. Or have I made this up? She says, "When you come on, you come on." We are in *Charade* where no one is who they say they are except perhaps for Audrey/Reggie. Or is she? She must deal with the changing names and perhaps personas of Cary/Peter, Adam, Brian. Have I got them all? Does it matter?

Isn't three the perfect number as identity is the question. Is it not always the question?

And the river shows the way as it journeys through the city beneath the 32, or is it 37 bridges?

Go to http://www.pariswater.com/ponts/ponts.htm where you can click for photos and pretend that you were with me: as I recall and as Paris is blanketed in morning snow.

Repair

Paris repairs. Consider the Hôtel de Ville, city hall, in the 4th arrondissement, a giant sand castle fantasy that dates from 1357 and is still the working center of the city. At night in winter, it sparkles like a dream come true.

Take the Metro to the station of that name or simply walk Rue de Rivoli. Start in Marais and follow that road all the way to the Louvre or further if you are going to eat at Le Zimmer.

Take the Metro to George V: Don't miss the Champs-Élysées at Christmas.

But walk this city.

The repairs will startle. The lining of my heavy black coat, its hem that touches the top of my boots, got caught on a boot link: separated and frayed. I could have walked into any dry cleaners along the streets of Marais and gotten an excellent repair. But it was Sunday. So I pinned the hem with safety pins and walked to the open market at Bastille: fresh food: roasted beets (yes, they roast them for you), cheese, meat, fish, a rabbit for dinner (Yes, I cooked it. See the recipe below.) But I also found needle and thread and so could do the repair myself. I am not the seamstress my mother was, nor as good as anyone in the Parisian dry cleaners, but the satisfaction of the needle and thread in hand healed.

Repair.

Paris dreams. For at night we repair through sleep and dreams. Parisians do not balk at movies and books with dreams. In Paris it is safe to dream. It is safe even to write about the dreams. Hélène Cixous wisely advises,

> Crossing the frontiers to the other world without transition, at the stroke of the signifier, this is what dreams permit us to do and why, if we are dreamers, we love dreams so much. It's the cancellation of opposition between inside and outside . . .

I go into the closet, hear a noise, perhaps the neighbors, I think, and lean closer to the wall to listen.

This is of course absurd in the way that dreams are.

From inside the closet, from the wall something touches my breast. I'm unable to move or see.

Paralyzed the way we sometimes are in dreams and in this case also blind.

I try to open my eyes but can't. And still I see. I am no longer the center of the picture. I am the observer. Someone else goes into the closet in the light and finds a box. In it is a large crude oddly shaped oboe. A musician decides to try to play the instrument. It is difficult at first but then he wets the reed with his tongue and the oboe responds to his mouth, his touch, and the sound becomes more compelling, the playing more necessary.

But then the oboe is lying on a bureau. It waits for him—like a demand: When will you be home? When will you play me?

I was hidden.

I lay alone in my bed in Paris and knew this: To be absent was how I dealt with D.'s inability to connect. "Only connect . . .", E.M. Forster tells us in the epigraph of *Howard's End*. How often I have read that line, spoken it. How deeply I thought I had understood when I had not. Yes, D. left me, but where was I?

When the light came late in the morning as it does in Paris in December, I walked the streets of Marais. There I stood somewhere in the 3rd or 4th before a repair shop for clarinets and oboes and saxophones and flutes . . .

If only I could paint this. Perhaps I will for the dream that moves from the wound to become something other than itself reinvents, repairs.

And I dream . . . without transition: hat trick, bedtrick, mind trick.

Here is Melissa Clark's wonderful recipe for Mustardy Braised Rabbit with Carrots.

Mustardy Braised Rabbit With Carrots

Time: 2 hours 45 minutes

A Good Appetite: Braised Rabbit, Easier on the Fat (*The New York Times,* February 4, 2009)
1/4 cup all-purpose flour
2 thyme sprigs
1 rosemary sprig
1 whole clove
1 2 1/2-pound rabbit, cut into 8 pieces, rinsed and patted dry
1 1/2 teaspoons kosher salt
1 1/2 teaspoons ground black pepper
1/4 cup (4 tablespoons) extra virgin olive oil
4 large leeks, halved lengthwise, cleaned and thinly sliced crosswise
3 tablespoons chopped fresh sage

1 pound carrots, peeled, trimmed and cut into 1 1/2-inch chunks
1 celery stick, diced
3 garlic cloves, thinly sliced
2 teaspoons whole coriander seeds
1 cup dry white wine
About 2 cups chicken stock
1 to 2 tablespoons Dijon mustard, to taste
2 tablespoons chopped fresh parsley, for garnish
Buttered noodles, for serving (optional).

1. Preheat oven to 325 degrees. Place flour in a shallow bowl. Tie thyme, rosemary and clove in a spice sachet or square of cheesecloth (or just toss them in pot if you do not mind accidentally biting into clove later).
2. Season rabbit pieces all over with salt and pepper. Coat each piece evenly with flour; tap off excess. Heat 3 tablespoons oil in a large oven-proof Dutch oven over medium-high heat. Sear rabbit in batches, until browned all over, 5 to 6 minutes a side. Transfer to a paper-towel-lined plate.
3. Add remaining 1 tablespoon oil to pot; reduce heat to medium. Add leeks and 2 tablespoons sage and cook, stirring, until softened, about 2 minutes. Stir in the carrots, celery, garlic, coriander, salt and pepper. Cook, stirring, until vegetables begin to color, about 5 minutes.
4. Add wine and increase heat to high; simmer, scraping up browned bits from bottom of pot, until reduced by half, about 5 minutes. Return rabbit to pot. Add stock (it should come almost halfway up the sides of rabbit) and herb sachet (or herbs and clove). Transfer pot to oven and cook, partially covered, until meat is fork tender, about 2 hours.
5. Transfer rabbit pieces to a serving platter. If liquid seems too thin, place pot over medium-high heat and simmer until it thickens slightly. Discard sachet. Stir in mustard, to taste. Spoon sauce and vegetables over rabbit. Garnish with parsley and remaining 1 tablespoon chopped sage. Serve with noodles, if desired.

The Last Place You Look

Music from a window in Paris, a pianist's ringing tones, notes cascading on the air like cartoon quarter notes slide down a music staff from the open window: I have walked from 7 Rue des Francs-Bourgeois along Pavée Payenne, stopped for a cappuccino at my favorite Café Sévigné at the corner of Rue du Parc Royal—not on the street of its name—and thought once again that nothing is what it seems. I did not turn onto Rue de Thorigny toward the Musée Picasso because it is closed for renovation until 2012, believe it or not. I was gifted with the music by choosing by chance (the museum closed) R. du Parc Royal: With the sound of D. that was not D. When I've been to Paris before, I *did* visit the Musée Picasso and loved its orderly chronology of his work that results in the disorderly invention that is his work as if chronology will reveal. But discovery does not come in order.

I recall an Angela Carter short story, the whorl of a shell gone wrong, as if we see it mirrored, no way to know what is what or who is who, "Reflections," from a book that sits on my shelf in my condo in D.C.

In Paris I'd begun to long for my book-lined condo with the exposed brick, the exposed duct work—air-conditioning and heating tubes that circle my flat. Carter's story, my apartment reflect recent memory: When D. left me, as I have said long ago here, I got out of town, went as a visiting writer, a low-level job actually, as I am not famous, at a distinguished writing department where no one noticed my existence, as if I actually did not exist. This sense of not being known fit as if I were on the other side of a mirror.

I have been lost.

I came to Paris, without transition, over water in a cold land (Paris in December). Once there I put my passport in a drawer and dreamed—hoped?— it might be nowhere to be found—no way to return.

Here's how I think of my passport: On the front is a picture of my father. My picture lies under his and under my mother's. Remembering from where I've come has helped. My father's love, my mother's love, my childhood with them lay inside that passport to my destination.

I've boarded a plane whose destination remains unknown. Inside the plane, stuffed chairs in fours, banquets, tables and chairs, the kitchen I lost. I look for a comfortable man, a man I know, a man who would let me lay my head on his shoulder to sleep, but that man is nowhere to be found.

A fantasy. A wish. As if I am in a strange tale of my own making.

While my daughter Sarah was pregnant with Lila, I dreamt that she was born and at barely a month she speaks, words and sentences that we can understand. She runs and I assure Sarah that a baby will not run more than a hundred feet from its mother. The baby knows not to let the parent out of sight. I think now that I dreamt this because I have known that letting go is first. We are born when let go.

I let D. go when I had no choice. And now that I do have choice, I have let him be gone. I am comforted that the music of his piano will drift from strangers' windows.

I have sat cold in Place des Voges to consider.

I have walked Marais to discover Le Marché des Enfants Rouges at 39 rue de Bretagne where I ate sardines and eel, drank green tea and returned to my apartment to sleep.

At 6:30 in the morning my cell phone rings and it is D. He is outside my apartment building's door. I give him the code to get in that door. My apartment looks out on a courtyard that he must pass. I stand in my filmy white cotton robe, white hair loose and mussed before the window that looks out on the courtyard and speak to him. He stands suitcase in hand. I say, "There is no room for you."

"May I come up?" he says.

"It's a lot of stairs."

"I'm good at stairs." He is standing below the window here in a doorway talking on his cell phone to mine.

We look at one another.

You may ask, How does he know where I am? Before I left, he suggested I give him my address in case of emergency. Seemed wise.

An emergency? No. We have lived through that.

He has brought gifts: Rom-Coms: *French Kiss, Charade, Something's Gotta Give.* He says he will go to a hotel post haste. He has packed lightly.

I let him stay.

My bed is a double bed and he is tired. We lie down and sleep. We do not make love. When we awake, we go to Café Sévigné for omelets, croissants and cappuccino. He tells me he has never left me. I beg to differ. He tells me that he was lost, that the time he's been away was a time to find, to search, to understand. He tells me he thought he would find a life that was separate from me but what he found instead was a life that was his and that did not fit anywhere without me.

We walk the day into an evening winter. Near midnight, smokers: couples, singles, the street made safe by a habit that is banned indoors. The light of the match, a young man smiling at his girlfriend as she tries again and again to get her smoke and the flame breathing as she breathes in.

What he will tell me and what I tell him is to be revealed, for time is needed to discover, but in Paris I learned this:

In what I imagine is their reflected light, I hear D.'s words and in the dark see on his chest a small box. It is a box that I have seen before but that box was locked. I used to think that some day *I* would find the key, for the key was lost. Now the box is open. Inside the box, his heart beats: open heart, open heart.

I have not had the key.

He has come to Paris by the route T.S. Eliot describes:

> To arrive where you are, to get from where you are
>
> not,
>
> You must go by a way wherein there is no ecstasy.
>
> In order to arrive at what you do not know
>
> You must go by a way which is the way of ignorance.
>
> In order to possess what you do not possess
>
> You must go by the way of dispossession.
>
> In order to arrive where you are not
>
> You must go through the way in which you are not.
>
> And what you do not know is the only thing you know
>
> And what you own is what you do not own
>
> And where you are is where you are not.

I have come to Paris this way.

We have met.

Where we've arrived is not on any map.

I now know the answer to this question: Where do you find what you have lost?

What Happens in Paris

Here is what D. and I did together in Paris. Read here for the joys of the light-hearted city full of lights. The bateau at night is incredible just as it is in *Charade*—well, okay not that incredible. After all I am not Audrey Hepburn but Cary: Peter/Brian/Adam has appeared.

And I have begun to know who is who.

We picked up the bateaux at Pont De L'Alma at 5 p.m. in the winter to see the sunset and then the Tour Eiffel in sparkling darkness at 6: the ride is short enough to not do you in, long enough to relax and the Paris you see from the Seine will fill your heart: Open heart, open heart. Take a look at:

http://www.bateaux-mouches.fr/

We had dinner at Brazzerie Zimmer.
(http://www.lezimmer.com/)

From the bateau, we walked up Avenue Georges V and caught the metro, the 1 line. To follow our path, get off at Chatelet, exit through the Place de Chatelet sortie and you are there. Eat the steak, the artichoke, drink Pomerol, try the Berthillon salted caramel ice cream. Bon apétit!

Breakfront

But, in Paris, despite the Rom-Com I appeared to be living, skepticism reared its head. I recalled a key line from the Richard Gere and Dianne Lane movie *Nights in Rodanthe.* Late nights in Paris, D. and I watched in bed on my laptop, the Rom-Coms I love that he'd brought as gifts. He did *not* bring *Nights in Rodanthe*.

I must admit *Nights in Rodanthe* is a truly awful flick with actors I adore. It is not nearly as good as *French Kiss*—that he *did* bring. *Nights in Rodanthe* lacks that film's edge of irony.

We are sleeping late in the a.m. so that D. can adjust to the time change and, I think now, because I've needed to sleep in the comfort of his embrace. So I sleep even more than usual. I have always slept like a lion.

But I *am* self-protective in Paris and for some time after Paris. My not-so-ironic self relies on that one line from *Nights in Rodanthe* to get at my deep problem: fear that he may leave me again. Did it once. Why not twice?

Spoiler here, so skip the next paragraph if you haven't seen *Nights in Rodanthe*. Oh, come on, read it anyway.

Nights in Rodanthe is not a Rom-Com. As I've said, in the true Rom-Com two cynics meet, neither believes love works, one or both have been hurt or been screwed by believing that the open heart is a good thing. So one, or in this case both, have closed off that option: closed heart, closed heart. In the Rom-Com, you do not kill off the hero. That's what happened in *Nights in Rodanthe*—to my horror, not my tears. Go figure, I felt betrayed by the film.

I have not wanted to *kill off* D., metaphorically, or G-d help me, literally. Thus, the open door, and open heart, despite all the breakage.

But betrayal—and there are many ways two people in a marriage may betray one another—is both my subject and my dilemma. Figuring out who is who and what is what inside my own head have been part and parcel of this journey—and I don't mean to Paris—or do I?

In my limp defense, I have asserted to D. too many times that I've been through great loss and years of uncertainty both during the marriage and the separation. Not that this makes me unique.

But taking D. back has been no easy process: I'm scared.

So, I quote to D. this line from the movie, "Any guy who would leave a woman like you—" I do love it when Gere says that to Lane. And at that moment in Paris and for some time after, I needed the line. I needed the answer.

D. interrupts, "Should have his head examined. No, wait—I did!" D. finally did go to a shrink and I think he's now fully shrunk—is that a word? I, on the other hand . . . Well, let's just say, My process continues.

D. adds, "I won't cop to being an idiot as in, 'Any guy who would leave a woman like you is an idiot.' I will cop to have my head examined—as in 'Any guy who . . ., needs to have his head examined.' "

I have been seeing a therapist through the whole writing of this memoir. In fact, there have been two. Kinda like two marriages—and I've had two of those as well. The first shrink Cynthia moved her practice to Wyoming. I cannot click my heels and be with her, but she did feel like *home.* With Cynthia I had what might have been the first truly intimate relationship in my life. For the first time, I came to understand something about being seen and that being seen constitutes intimacy.

Do you remember in *Bridget Jones's Diary* when Mark Darcy tells Bridget something like this, "I like you just as you are"? That's the Rom-Com version of what I have come to discover. Intimacy lies somewhere in that line of dialogue that amazes all of Bridget's friends.

My second therapist, who has walked on this road with me is Martha.

Cynthia has worked with her and made certain that I saw her before Cynthia moved away—to be sure about the fit. Martha is less formidable or perhaps I am further on the road. Cynthia was a bit scary. Therapy is no easy process though it gets lampooned and satirized and rightfully so, with Woody Allen doing the best work on solipsism in life and in film.

But the real stuff has, I think anyway, little to do with navel gazing.

Martha has shown me the way to the yellow brick road and I have seen that there is no Wizard behind the curtain. Like the Scarecrow with no brain, the Tinman with no heart, the Cowardly Lion with no courage, I have been at a loss. But like them, I have learned that the Wizard lies within and that I am no wizard.

I can't find my way alone. I have needed and sought help. I have been afraid.

Before I went to Paris, once I'd found the apartment, rented it, bought the plane ticket, and even had Euros, I went into an unexplained panic. My friend Marly said to me, "Mary, you've done everything. You even have your Euros. Now's the time for anticipation." It was a week before the trip. "Something new and different is about to happen to you." I said, "Right, I'll get lost or be robbed. But here's the thing, my getting lost is not a new and different thing." For almost a year while commuting back and forth to Missouri, I walked out my front door here at my D.C. condo and regularly got lost. Sense of direction in the literal and figurative sense is not my strong suit. So I said to Marly, "The new thing is that now I'm down to being robbed."

What was that about? Certainly not logical thinking.

So I did what I always do when I can't figure something out. I slept. I had this dream about sex and storage. Oh so you don't think these two are related? I beg to differ:

In the dream, I wake wanting to make love but don't say anything. D. does too and comes towards me, penis erect. I want his penis inside but he doesn't want to enter because he says he wants to experiment. He wants my vibrator.

I am dreaming of the vibrator that I have had since D. left me, that never would have been possible for me to have while we were together. Because of our problems with sex—his rejection of me?—I assumed, incorrectly I now know, that he would have been offended by it.

So in the dream, when I reach into the side table at my bedside where I keep it when I'm awake, I have instead the side table from the bedroom set that belonged to my first husband and me, the one table from that set that I took when we divorced. Yeah, yeah, I know: Two strikes and you're . . .

The vibrator is not in the side table. It is empty.

I live in a small condo with very little storage. When California Closets helped me create more storage, I still had to throw away many prized items I no longer had room for, mostly books—and that, the loss of a book I have read is a difficulty I've not been able to overcome—I could live in a library. I was able to save parts of clown costumes I'd made when my children were small and D. took home the clown costume I had made for him, but I couldn't find my pink gingham clown costume. When my children were small I made all the costumes in different colors of gingham. D.'s was green. Sarah's was red. Ben's was blue. Sarah and Ben are, if I've not made this clear before, the children from my first failed marriage.

In the dream, my clown costume was in the long bureau from that bedroom set, long gone, sold at the sale of our house in Adams Morgan: the four-story Victorian brownstone. In the dream I found this bureau with its ridged top slider for jewelry and underneath, crayons and small blocks, small toys for children. (I have a brand new grandchild, Lila.)

Then I find my mother's breakfront that ended up in the basement of the house before Kalorama, the house in Chevy Chase, the colonial that I loved where we bought my first mahogany dining room set that we took with us to the dining room in the old Victorian that dwarfed a console piano—that's how big the room was: a room where all my children and grandchildren could come to eat the food I once cooked in my chef's kitchen. D. sold that mahogany table after I went to Missouri to teach, after he'd decided to leave me, after we'd sold the house.

I have seen mahogany trees in St. Lucia, an island of beaches and rainforests and a dark people with open hearts.

In the dream, the mahogany breakfront's first drawer had a silver drawer like the one in my sideboard where I stored my mother's sterling that my father gave me after she died. That sideboard D. also sold after I'd flown away to Missouri to teach fiction writing as a visiting writer. My first book had just come out. No book party. No sixtieth birthday party. Yes, my publisher sent the first copies out on my birthday, March 3. But there was no celebration. There was instead as my father said after D. and I took him, after my mother and sister had both died, to his first James Bond movie, "A lot of breakage."

One night after we'd gotten back to D.C., while I was washing my face—D. slept over—I said, "You know what you gave me?"

"What?"

"You gave me a window into my soul and then you took it away. I know inside that I should be able to find my own window into my own soul. Isn't that what all the therapy has been about?"

He listened.

I continued, "Aren't two people afraid stronger than one afraid and doesn't the human connection of love—and I mean committed, sexual love—manifest G-d?"

Did I really say that? Yeah, I did. And I believe it, but it hasn't been an easy thing to say aloud.

And D. spoke, "Maybe I just borrowed the window for a while."

Here is something you do not know. D. has been reading this memoir the whole time I have been writing it—as a blog that now is this book you are reading.

I was often afraid to post the chapters of what was a "live" memoir on the blog. Great anxiety accompanied "posting." Overcoming that fear has been part of being *seen*.

D. told me he'd been reading the blog when we were in Paris. I told him how afraid I have been.

"Think about Confucius," he said. "Out of all the pain and craziness in the world, he got an enormous amount of material." He has a wit that charmed me from the get-go.

I said, and here we see that I am *not* funny, "Confucius say: Confusion create pain in soul."

But confusion does guide. This I have learned.

The bottom dropped out of my world much the way the bottom dropped out of the stock market with what is now known as The Great Recession that President Obama inherited. I mention Obama because he and Michelle appear to me to be the real thing: A true romance.

When that bottom hit and we all got hit, I wrote this to D., not realizing at the time that my subject was our marriage:

We must lead with our hearts and not our minds. I know this seems antithetical to what we are hearing in the news about how we should respond with reason to the crash, but let us not be held bondage to the intellect, which on some level says, all is lost. Let us lead with our hearts—not emotion, not feeling—but our hearts that know that we shall weather this together and that we will hang in when all seems lost and hopeless and the bottom has dropped out. Because we believe that, to be trite but true, love is the answer even in the face of a market that appears to offer little hope. We do live in a forgiving cosmos even when all seems lost.

And D. wrote back to me:

As usual, you speak goodness that must be the true guide to all of us who live in the practical world.

Whether or not you agree with me about The Great Recession, you may understand what I mean when I say that D. *sees* me.

John L. Hitchcock, physicist and Jungian analyst in his book *At Home in the Universe: Re-envisioning the Cosmos with the Heart*, says:

This book is a declaration of love. It is not a declaration of *my* love, but of the fact that love is the heart of the universe . . . [I]t is we who submit to the bonds of love. And since love sets its object free—since love is the very basis of our freedom—in submitting to its bonds, we also set free whomever or whatever is the object of our love. In a profound sense. . . submitting to the bonds of love can help release even God. We can love reality as it is, though it seems to throw obstacles in our way and wound us.

I long ago let D. go. By reading this memoir while I wrote it, D. let *me* go. And I have been freed and *seen*.

Our marriage that was broken has had a solidity I could never have imagined. It is like a mahogany breakfront that holds all the broken china of our lives together.

Derek Walcott who won the Nobel Prize for literature in 1992, the year before my sister died, the year before we took my father to that James Bond film, was born and raised in St. Lucia, the isle of indestructible mahogany. In his Nobel acceptance speech, he said, *Break a vase and the love that reassembles the fragments is stronger than that love which took its symmetry for granted when it was whole.*

You Cannot Get Out of the Game

While I was dating, while the process of discovery unfolded, before Paris, D. sent me an article about the winemaker we'd met on a vacation to Napa: Soter's winery is Etude: a word that evokes memory and music and a type of composition that was sometimes written as an exercise: to learn from.

That's what we've been doing, creating an etude.

Over a glass of wine in Paris at Café Sevigny, after I'd let him into my apartment, after we'd spent a week together, walking the streets of Paris, D. said to me, "Mary, I look at you and I see your heart. You lead with your heart. Even into battle, you lead, fearless, with your heart. The world sees, but does not understand. Your brave little heart is bruised and hurt. But again you lead with your heart, and again, and again. I want to be the person who protects that heart."

I don't simply recall this. I now have it in writing because I recently asked him if he recalled that moment and instead of simply answering, "Yes," he wrote what you have just read and sent it to me.

It is almost as if he has been in my corner while I battled the world as a single woman, new to the venue.

Back home in D.C. after Paris, we made love after a ballet performance at the Kennedy Center where I have season tickets, where I have gone alone, treated myself to a box seat. He bought a ticket in the orchestra where he could look up and see me. The ballet does not matter, but I would have liked for it to have been Stravinsky's *The Firebird*, which I have seen though not with D. My favorite is the choreography by Balanchine because Stravinsky and Balanchine knew each other and collaborated. Chagall did the sets that I have only seen in photos after the two reshaped the ballet for its premiere in November 1949, the year of D.'s birth, for the New York City Ballet.
http://www.auburn.edu/~mitrege/russian/art/chagall-firebird.html

Stravinsky wrote the first version of *The Firebird* in 1910 when he worked with the choreographer Fokine who held the reins—an unsatisfying relationship that would inform Stravinsky. With Balanchine, something new and separate arose from what has been viewed as a true collaboration: music and dance: Stravinsky, so involved that he conducted the 1949 premiere. Is there anyway to perceive with exactitude what each contributed to the partnership? How the music affected the dance? Or was it the other way around? It is said the result was like nothing ever seen before.

D. with his perfect pitch often speaks of the inability of recorded music to ever exactly reproduce the same sound waves as live instruments. He is also schooled in the sciences. I suspect that he might assert, It's an impossibility the way reaching absolute zero, the temperature at which all motion down to and including the subatomic level ceases, is impossible to reach despite the fact that it is a fixed and precisely known temperature and the object of much modern-day effort to achieve a laboratory reading as close to it as possible. This, the Third Law of Thermodynamics, seems to me an apt metaphor for the inability of a recording to reproduce exactly.

Similarly, if events can be said to have occurred in an exact manner, perception can never capture that exactitude. I put it this way: I recall the events that happened between me and D. but I will not "reach absolute zero" in the telling, let alone in my understanding of *why* he left me.

I remember when I lay in bed and cried over the Second Law of Thermodynamics. I said to D., "That's my problem. I'm going to entropy." My marriage had broken. D. had said, "I need to be alone."

But here's the thing, he stayed in the game, pursuing the elusive me while I dreamed of the elusive D. He says I come to him in fire and music. He says he's no hero. But I beg to differ because he has had the etude of our dance in his head.

I listen to *The Firebird*. Stravinsky switches between the ominous themes in minor keys and the glorious themes in major keys, with large variations in volume for both, much of it played at the extremes. These forces struggle throughout for the upper hand, and the outcome is not clear until the end like a good movie. While we generally know which is which (ominous and glorious), things get complicated. Some of the quieter glorious passages have an ominous undertone. Some instruments serve as an "instrument" of the ominous at some points and the glorious at others. There are some steady voices—the horns repeatedly sounding caution; the oboe as the only consistent (almost without exception) expression of hope.

It's like the movie *North by Northwest*, which is not so different from *The Firebird*—all tug between good and bad, with the good guys and bad guys clearly drawn. Deep down, we know who is who even when it seems we don't. The only thing we don't know is who will prevail (theoretically, if you put aside the fact that it's Cary Grant).

A frantic battle ensues—this is pretty late in the piece—the fifth section; the sections are short and the whole piece is only forty-one minutes, twelve seconds. The next scene moves into a lush melody with a strong hint of foreboding, or even despair, with cries and pleas from solo instruments.

Now that I have found the Paris that is not on any map and the one that is, now that I have been through a long process of self-discovery that is far from over, logic tells me the Laws of Thermodynamics rule.

Once, when we had that chef's kitchen, D. complained that the new dishwasher—a German-made product that supposedly was built to last—wouldn't drain, "The damn thing is two years old and broken." I laughed and said, "You forget the Second Law of Thermodynamics."

On the day I wept, when the marriage was broken, before I got in that cab with my one large suitcase and flew away to Missouri, he said at the side of the bed where I lay in despair, "But you forget the First Law, the Conservation of Energy: Energy can be neither created or destroyed."

I didn't understand.

I only understand this—and it has been a long time coming: The only path D. could follow was to leave to discover himself. But he never forgot the Laws of Thermodynamics.

C.P. Snow provided this shorthand to remember the laws: 1. You cannot win. 2. You cannot break even. 3. You cannot get out of the game.

But if you stay in the game, you can dance even when it seems that the dancers have all gone under the hill.

Lost and Found

I scroll through the Rom-Coms on my shelf—I originally mistyped *self*—the unconscious mind has a mind of its own. In this memoir that I wrote "live," meaning while I was living it, I've mulled over, written about, dreamed of: *When Harry Met Sally, Four Weddings and a Funeral, Hitch, Something's Gotta Give, Baby Boom, Holiday, A Man and a Woman, P.S. I love You, Juno, The Thomas Crown Affair*—or TCA—as D. refers to that one because of the number of times I've watched it—*French Kiss, Green Card, While You Were Sleeping, The Proposal.* Have I got them all?

No: *Charade.* How do we know who is who?

Charade's trailer features an aging Cary Grant in voice-over speaking of Regina Lampert played by the young Audrey Hepburn. He oozes irony as he says, "Her life was one round of enjoyment, entertainment, enchantment?" And his voice rises with the sound a question mark makes as Audrey screams at the sight of the man, played viciously by George Kennedy, with a hook for a hand. "She was in serious trouble, but she still knew how to enjoy herself. You see, it all began when he fell off the train." Regina's husband Charles is quite dead. "Now there's a relaxed husband," opines Cary. "Police probably think I killed him," Audrey says, quite seriously. "Instant divorce, you mean?" Cary replies.

When I began this memoir, I thought my writing might in some way *disappear* D. At least, I'd get divorced. I did get legally separated. The documents are signed. I could, if D. and I could resist making love for six months, simply walk into a D.C. courtroom with my attorney and get a divorce.

Instead, D. took me on a road trip. He told me to pack a bag with something to wear to dinner. I dressed in jeans, a sweater and wore the coat with the repaired hem. I do have a dress coat that flares at the hem and has a soft rim of fur on the collar and cuffs.

But who knew where we were going?

Not me, and D. wasn't telling. Instead, he says, "I have music," as he connects his iPod to his car radio.

When we were together before the breakage, D. used to complain that I was always playing Leonard Cohen while I cooked in that chef's kitchen in my old lady of a house. "What is all that droning?" he'd ask before he got to know Leonard during our separation. I remember going alone to the documentary *Leonard Cohen, I'm Your Man* at the E Street theater not far from where my D.C. condo now sits. I remember meeting D. afterwards at Bistro D'Oc on 10th Street, NW. I just couldn't sit there with him—this man who was selling the house.

The houses are all gone under the sea.

I walked out after I ate Bistro D'Oc's lovely paté, took the metro to Dupont Circle, walked home to Adams Morgan, put the key for one of the last times into the lock of the old Victorian lady and went to bed alone. We were no longer sleeping in the same bed.

D. got to know Leonard well over the last four years of our separation. This, among a whole lot more, I have learned.

He makes his way down Constitution Avenue and before I know it we are on I-66 going towards Virginia: Leonard Cohen's "Cheslea Hotel" and "Everybody Knows" sung by Rufus Wainwright plays. Then "Tonight Will Be Fine" and "The Future" sung by Teddy Thompson.

This road trip has a soundtrack.

When K.D. Lang begins to belt out "Helpless," Neil Young's heartbreaker of a song, the roadside looks familiar. I know where I am through eidetic memory. I recall a trip down this road when I was fifty and going off to grad school. D. took me away to celebrate my leap from corporate America to college, to write.

. . . though it may look like (*Write* it!) disaster.

I recall the framed photo D. gave me that he extracted from my father's eight millimeter home movie of me at maybe six years old wearing my Davy Crockett buckskin jacket, standing in front of the stoop at the rowhouse on Grantley Road. All my father's movies were of the little girls, my sister and me, coming out of the front door in pea coats or new dresses. There I am with my arms out, ready to spin—the photo is fuzzy.

D. said as he handed the photo to me: "Here's the real Mary Tabor," as if I were on *To Tell the Truth*: "Will the real Mary Tabor please stand up."

In the car, I now know where we're going or think I do. I say, "You better know what you're doing."

He says, "You think?"

As he turns into the Howard Johnsons Motel in Warrenton, Virginia, Perla Batalla is singing Leonard Cohen's "Bird on a Wire," and I begin to laugh and cry. This is not where we are going but it *is* a shared memory. Once D. and I went to Sarasota, Florida to visit his aunt and uncle with D.'s parents. D. wanted to save money and we stayed in an un-refurbished-fifties-maybe

Howard Johnsons on a strip filled with decrepit buildings. We had a horror of a bathroom and bed. I wanted to sleep with my clothes on, wouldn't take off my socks to walk on the dirty carpet and bathroom linoleum.

"I know where we're going."

"Do you now?" He backs up the car, makes the right turn toward Washington, Virginia, and we sing with Jarvis Crocker Leonard's "If It Be Your Will." We are on the way to The Inn at Little Washington.

http://www.theinnatlittlewashington.com/

When he turns into the parking space under the four flags, we are singing Leonard's "Anthem," my favorite Leonard Cohen song and it is snowing. We are singing with Julie Christensen and Martha Wainright.

I am struck dumb when I am greeted by name at the inn. My coat is taken. "I would have worn a better coat if I'd known we were coming here." The concierge and D. smile at one another.

We are taken to tea. I finger the love bird ring on my right hand, an antique ring he gave me many, many years ago, and tell him, "This ring says it all."

"Does it now?"

And then we are escorted to the Game Keeper's Cottage.

I am *not* making this up.

I say to the concierge, "This is right out of D.H. Lawrence!" He and D. smile again.

His photo of the cottage here, taken the next morning when the snow had melted, is slightly crooked, but then so is the truth.

The fire is burning. And there are bags. A lot of sacks. And one great big one. He hands me the first gold sack: In it is an envelope and a book wrapped in gold paper. I open the envelope.

D. has hand colored the dragonfly illustration—I use the dragonfly on my Mac to identify me in e-mail. What follows is typed and written on parchment like a poem. See the photo of it, but here are the words:

My Dearest Mary,
I once thought I didn't believe in signs.
Or, at most, they are so exceedingly rare,
And even then, so easily explained by the rational crutch of

coincidence.

But sometimes a sign is so powerful and perfectly timed as to leave one dumbstruck,

with no rational explanation, laughing derisively at the possibility of coincidence.

We were one year into the separation.

I was reading this copy of *On Chesil Beach*—a book that affected me deeply—on a flight returning to DC from Iowa. I had just read a particular passage that stuck in my mind, then I reached for my ticket stub to use as a bookmark.

As I put it in the page, I saw, stopped, stared. And knew.

I will lead your applause.

And then in his turquoise-ink print:

My love forever,

D. (see p. 152)

My Dearest Mary,

I once thought I didn't believe in signs.
Or, at most, they are so exceedingly rare,
and even then, so easily explained by the rational crutch of coincidence.

But sometimes a sign is so powerful and perfectly timed as to leave one dumbstruck,
with no rational explanation, laughing derisively at the possibility of coincidence.

We were one year into the separation.
I was reading this copy of *On Chesil Beach* – a book that affected me deeply – on a flight returning to DC from Iowa.
I had just read a particular passage that stuck in my mind, then I reached for my ticket stub to use as a bookmark.
As I put it in the page, I saw, stopped, stared. And knew.

I will lead your applause.

My love forever,
D.
(see p. 152)

I unwrap and open Ian McEwan's *On Chesil Beach*, a book I read as soon as it was published and he knows I have read it. I turn to the page: The passage is framed in turquoise ink and refers to the time when Florence and Edward visited Wigmore Hall where Florence hoped some day she would play her violin and where Edward vowed that he would be there in seat 9C to lead the applause.

D.'s note says, "See p. 199."

On page 199, I find in D.'s turquoise ink a framed passage that describes Edward many years later alone and the first violinist Florence who waits for the house lights to go up and looks to see who sits in seat 9C.

And there is D.'s note: "See next page."

On it is the stub from his Midwest Airlines flight to Kansas City, where he'd gone to visit his son after visiting his parents in Iowa, and on the stub is his seat number: **9C.**

Even in his sixties, a large, stout man with receding white hair and a pink, healthy face, he
kept up the ... k in
the avenue ... he
would take ... ild-
flowers on ... the
butterflies ... , re-
turning th ... hill
church, wh ... day
be buried. ... fork-
ing of the ... idly
think that t ... d to
consult her ... d he
would ima ... and
forty years ... he
would paus ... and
wonder whether this was where she stopped to
eat her orange. At last he could admit to himself
that he had never met anyone he loved as much,
found anyone, man or woman,

MIDWEST AIRLINES
BOARDING PASS

NAME OF PASSENGER
PERSINGER/ARDELL
MIDWEST MILES NUMBER
XXXXX1843
KANSAS CITY INTL
WASHINGTON REAGAN
MIDWEST AIRLINES

CARRIER - FLIGHT — CLASS - DATE — TIME
YX 99 R 27AUG130P
GATE 23 BOARDING TIME 100P SEAT SMOKE NO
ELECTRONIC

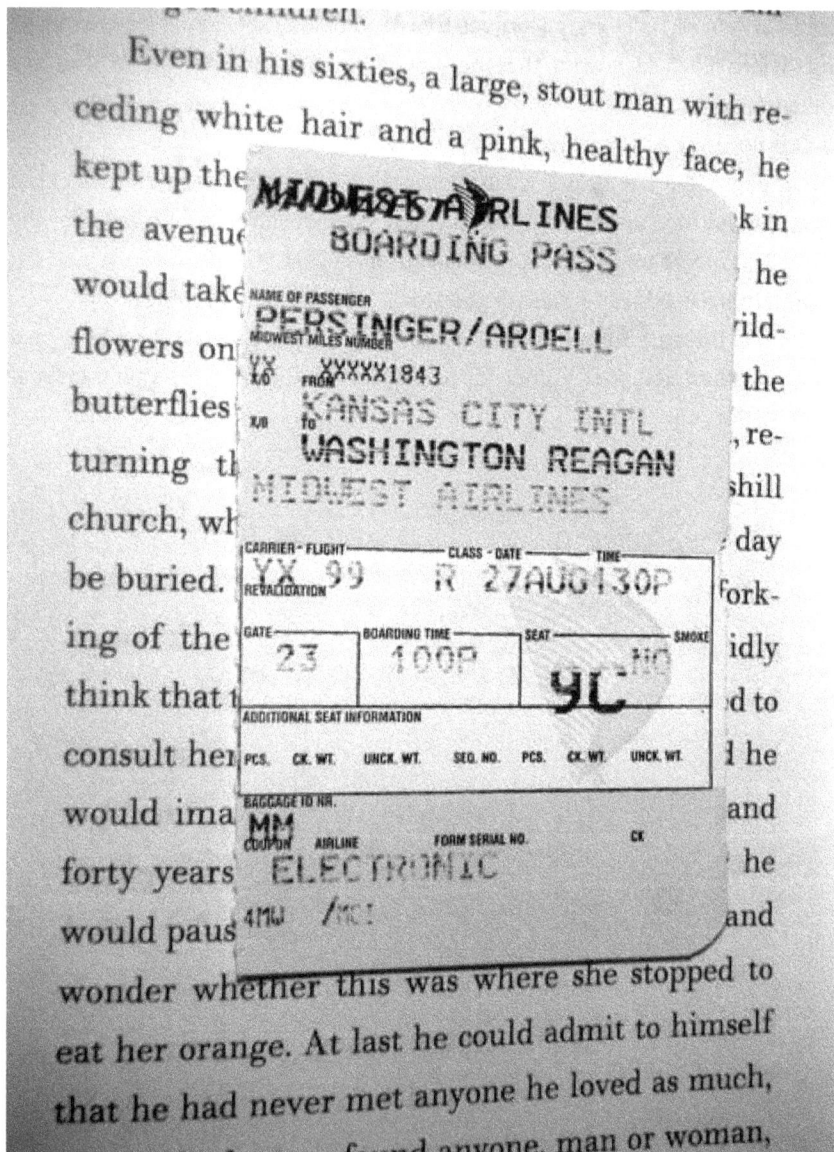

What follows: More boxes. One great big one, and some five more inside,
until I come to the little box that holds an antique diamond ring. And the man
to whom I am still legally married proposes to me, "Will you, love of my life,
marry me?"

We make love and then run into the open snowy field bundled in our coats,
our history and our hope.

I fear ending this memoir. If D. could leave me when I write, I think irrationally, he could leave me when I stop. He has always been *reading* me.

Scheherazade wrote to save her life. The old tale is that the Persian king after his wife betrayed him, married a virgin every night and killed her in the morning—until Scheherazade entranced him with her stories. http://www.gutenberg.org/files/19860/19860-h/19860-h.htm#THE_ARABIAN_NIGHTS

I have written this memoir to *find*.

D. says to me, "I was lost. Now I'm found."

I was *not* the answer. What he has told me is that he read twenty-two books of fiction the year I was in Missouri. D. is not a fiction reader, as a general rule.

But we are no longer about rules.

He said he read because he had much to learn about love.

I have been reading all my life, but I have learned that biblio-therapy goes only so far. I have been on a search and that search continues.

But I do know this: I have been found.

In the movie *Charade*, Audrey names at the end all the names that Cary has used in the movie. Whoever he is, she loves him.

I now know who D. is and I love him.

D.'s shrink P. said to him one day while he was still in therapy, "You've built the boat. You now want to learn how to sail it."

Can we live in a boat when *all the houses are gone under the sea?*

I dream houses on the sea. But the sea is a circle of sand filled by sea water bordered by large houses, each different. D. and I rent one of the houses. It comes with the house in town we own: We don't know how but we have it. It is like a memory of all the years we spent in Bethany Beach with the children, but it is not that place. It is not on any map. Two older women, sisters we guess, own the house nearby and we watch them wander together down to the sea. The air is warm. We go down to the sand and, where there were rocks, the tide has come in and pushed up soft sand all along the edges of the water. We go in, slide into sand and water, protected in the Caribbean bath-sea. There is ocean but no ocean. The sky above is terraced with lime green grass. We look up and see men and women, hair flowing, tanned legs astride thoroughbred horses. We have found protected sand and sea and sky—sheets of blue, kicked up by sea-blown wind.

And D. says to me, "You gotta build the house for the right reason."

I do not know how to fly, but I have in my heart the lightness of a bird.

Epilogue

A Message From My Heart:

Oddly enough, this book would not have happened if D. had not left me and sent me on my journey.

It would never have happened if Sarah Hammerschlag, my daughter, the philosopher and professor at Williams College, whose book *The Figural Jew: Politics and Identity in Postwar French Thought* published by University of Chicago Press in May 2010 (hurray! And it is brilliant.) and her husband, the philosopher and professor at University of Chicago, Ryan Coyne, had not suggested that I write about my journey while I lived it. They said, "Blog," while I wept, and I did. They wrote the first line of the blog that became this memoir: The title! I am in their debt forevermore for this, but more, indeed, for their incomparable love.

You can find her book at:

http://www.press.uchicago.edu/ucp/books/book/chicago/F/bo8374152.html

I thank my son Ben Hammerschlag, who is the owner and CEO of Epicurean Wines at http://www.epicureanwines.com (Here's one rec: if you haven't tried his personally designed wine Woop Woop, do so—a fabulous bottle of fine red wine for an unbelievably low price) and who spent many hours on the phone with me—as did my daughter and son-in-law—when the separation from D. happened, and who, as I write about in "Oz" in these pages, flew me to Australia where he owns a vineyard so that I could rest and recover and think about the state of my life. He is an incomparable man. I am blessed to know him.

From my heart, this thank you to my children—Sarah, Ben and Ryan—comes.

A special thank you to my grandson Jericho. Jericho at age 15 gave me advice that I will talk about more at a later time. Jericho is wise beyond his years. He is the son of Chris who held my hand when his father left me—what an unbelievable man Chris is. His wife Jessica and her daughter Madisson have stood by me, have been steadfast and true. And, believe it or not, the whole clan in Iowa stood by me, with a special salute here to Retha and Macel, who wrote me when the going was so rough and I didn't ever think I would recover.

I could never have written this memoir if I'd not gone to University of Missouri-Columbia as a visiting writer where I met the incredible writer and deeply empathic soul Marly Swick. Marly has been in my corner from the get-go. I made a friend for life and that alone is worth everything.

Sarah Krouse, who I once taught fiction writing to at George Washington University, taught me everything I know about blogging. She read and reread every chapter of this memoir. She is a brilliant mind, a soulful friend. She ought to be a literary agent—her advice has been invaluable, her friendship, a gift.

Jessica DeSorio Dalton of CitizensofDesign.com designed my website, got the blog up and running for me, taught me how to post, but more important, how to live fully.

Zaara of Kittenchops.com illustrated both my website and the blog and she did both with her heart after reading both my book *The Woman Who Never Cooked* and early writings of this memoir—she illustrated from understanding who I am and what I write. Her illustrations grace the cover and appear inside this book with her permission.

CitizensofDesign at http://www.citizensofdesign.com and Kittenchops at http://www.kittenchops.com are folks you need to know.

Amy Souza, whom I once taught—never underestimate what your students will teach you—asked me to participate in her project Spark at http://artspark.wordpress.com/ while I was living and discovering this memoir by blogging. I did and told her and the painters, writers and photographers this: "I'm a softy recovering from a broken heart. Long story. But let's just say that Amy's project offers me some hope for fixin' that heart through the work." Thank you, Amy.

Two photos by the professional photographer, Andy Duback, at http://www.andyduback.com whom I worked with twice on Spark, appear in this book with Andy's permission: Thank you, Andy.

To Cynthia Stevens and Martha Dupêcher: Much more ought to be said. For now, know that the journey of discovery continues. Cynthia Stevens, you were my first teacher on this path and together we walked. Martha Dupêcher, you have walked with me in the intimacy and safety of your wisdom and your heart.

What I've learned while writing this has come from the discovery that taking the risk of writing gifts—and I use that word *gifts* literally. As Elizabeth Bishop so wisely advises,

> —Even losing you (the joking voice, a gesture
> I love) I shan't have lied. It's evident
> the art of losing's not too hard to master
> though it may look like (*Write* it!) like disaster.

But, dear blog readers, your comments have informed these pages more than you know. I have read your comments and you have become part and parcel of this book. You have commented. I have rethought, been encouraged, forged ahead like a little boat on the sea of your belief.

This message comes from my heart to yours,

Mary

Mary

About the Author

Mary L. Tabor is the author of *The Woman Who Never Cooked*, which won Mid-List Press's First Series Award and was published when she was 60.

Her short stories have won numerous literary awards. Her experience spans the worlds of journalism, business, education, fiction and memoir writing.

She was a high school English teacher who joined the business world, leaving her corporate job when she was 50 to earn an MFA degree. She teaches at George Washington University, works with less-privileged populations at the D.C. library on how to get started writing, and is a Woodrow Wilson Visiting Fellow. She lives in the Penn Quarter in downtown D.C.

Also by Mary L. Tabor

The Woman Who Never Cooked: Stories
(First Series: Short Fiction)
The American adult woman is featured in
this debut collection of stories about love,
adultery, marriage, passion, death, and
family. Available on Amazon, Barnes &
Noble and other fine bookstores.

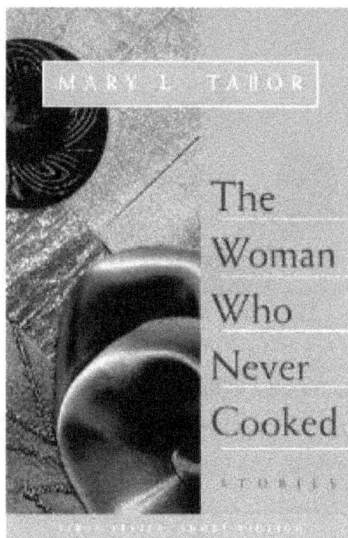

Mary L. Tabor

PERMISSIONS ACKNOWLEDGMENTS

Grateful acknowledgment is made to the following for permission to reprint previously published material.

D.H. Lawrence: excerpt of *"Kisses in the Train," from THE COMPLETE POEMS OF D.H. LAWRENCE by D.H. Lawrence,* edited by V. de Sola Pinto & F. W. Roberts, copyright (c) 1964, 1971 by Angelo Favagli and C. M. Weekley, Executors of the Estate of Frieda Lawrence Ravagli. Used by permission of Viking Penguin, a division of Penguin Group (USA) Inc.

Wendy Doniger: Excerpt from *The Bedtrick, Tales of Sex & Masquerade*, University of Chicago Press, 2000, by permission of the author.

Salman Akhtar: Excerpt from *Broken Structures: Severe Personality Disorders and Their Treatment.* Copyright 1992 by Jason Aronson, Inc. Reprinted by permission of Rowman & Littlefield Publishing Group.

Maurice Blanchot: Excerpt reprinted from *The Writing of the Disaster* by Maurice Blanchot, translated by Ann Smock, by permission of the University of Nebraska Press. Copyright 1986 by the University of Nebraska Press.

John Hitchcock: Except from *At Home in the Universe: Re-envisioning the Cosmos with the Heart* by John Hitchcock (West Chester, PA: Chrysalis Books, 2001) appears courtesy of the Swedenborg Foundation.

Dana Gioia: Excerpt of "Voyeur," from *Interrogations at Noon*, 2001 Graywolf Press, by permission of the author.

John Updike: Excerpt from *Self-Consciousness*, First Ballantine Books Edition, NY, 1990, deemed fair use by Random House, Inc.

E. E. Cummings: The lines from: "since feeling is first". Copyright 1926, 1954, © 1991 by the Trustees for the E. E. Cummings Trust. Copyright © 1985 by George James Firmage, from *Complete Poems: 1904-1962* by E. E. Cummings, edited by George J. Firmage. Used by permission of Liverwright Publishing Corporation.

Ethel Spector Person: Excerpt from *Dreams of Love and Fateful Encounters: The Power of Romantic Passion*, W. W. Norton & Company, Inc., 1988. Reprinted with permission from *Dreams of Love and Fateful Encounters* (Copyright 2007) American Psychiatric Publishing, Inc.

James Hollis: Excerpt from *The Middle Passage: From Misery to Meaning in Midlife*, Inner City Books, copyright 1993. Reprinted with permission of Daryl Sharp, publisher, Inner City Books.

www.ingramcontent.com/pod-product-compliance
Lightning Source LLC
Chambersburg PA
CBHW022106280326
41933CB00007B/271

* 9 7 8 0 9 8 2 9 9 3 1 7 0 *